FASHION FILES
Designers ^{FF}

MARIA COSTANTINO

BT Batsford Ltd London

© Maria Costantino 1997
First published 1997

Printed in Singapore
for the publishers
B T Batsford Ltd
583 Fulham Road
London SW6 5BY

http://www.batsford.com

ISBN 0 7134 8181 1

A CIP catalogue record for this book
is available from the British Library.

CONTENTS

INTRODUCTION

The fashion designer is a relatively recent phenomenon. As a professional designation, the title is unspecific for it covers both *haute couture* (high fashion) and *prêt-à-porter* (ready-to-wear). Now, increasingly, the designers are more celebrated than the clothes they create.

Couture simply means the dressmaking of garments made-to-measure for a private customer. First, clients visit the salon to view sample garments. Then, when they order a particular outfit from the range, it will be made up in their exact measurements, which may involve two or three fittings. The actual making of a *couture* garment usually takes several weeks.

Couture began in France. The first known *couturier* was Rose Bertin, dressmaker to Marie Antoinette who made her official court minister of fashion. The abdication of Emperor Napoleon III and the subsequent end of the French monarchy as arbiters of taste meant that wealthy clients came to rely more and more on their *couturiers'* judgement about styling and fashions. *Couturiers* became not only creative forces but business people directing workforces of seamstresses, tailors, mannequins and *vendeuses*.

Ironically it was an Englishman who was to become the founder of modern *couture*. Charles Worth (1825-95) was the first successful independent designer and the first to put his signature on his clothes, both, literally, on the label and by the creation of clothes that were directly attributable in style to him. Of equal importance is the fact that Worth was the first *couturier* to 'impose' his taste on his clients: previously the client had dictated their wishes to the dressmaker and the relationship was the traditional one of 'patron' and hired worker. Worth's back-draped flattened crinoline was the first silhouette to be introduced by an individual designer. To launch his new styles he required assistance from his wife or a prominent personality at court.

With their increasing social acceptance, *couturiers* could now dictate fashion more forcibly. Designers' understanding of the changing roles and needs of their clients became integral to their work. Since the First World War,

English-born Charles Worth (1825-95), the founder of modern *couture*, was the first to put a signature on clothes, adding a label bearing his name and creating designs whose style was directly attributable to him.

with more women entering the workforce, designers have had to react to women's growing financial and social independence. Increasingly *couturiers* have had to respond to a clientele that includes women from all over the world who have different canons of beauty, different social practices and different tastes. Today it is estimated that the Middle East accounts for at least 10 per cent of the fashion industry's world market. The constantly shifting profile of their clients led *couturiers* in the 1930s to experiment with boutique lines – individual items of clothing and accessories – as they faced increasing competition from the ready-to-wear clothing industry. By the 1960s, many *couturiers*, under siege from youth culture and fashion, found that the profits from *couture* were shrinking to almost nothing.

DEFINING A COUTURIER

In France today, the right to the title of *couturier* is in the gift of the *Chambre Syndicale de la Couture Parisienne*. In order to qualify for even being considered for official classification, a *couturier* must fulfil a number of criteria. First, *couturiers* must maintain at least one *atelier* (workshop) in Paris: these are largely centred in the Avenue Montaigne and the Faubourg Saint-Honoré. Second, the *atelier* must employ at least fifteen full-time technical staff, not including the director. For some smaller *couture* houses, this minimum staff number is a heavy financial burden and there is constant debate as to what constitutes 'full-time'. By contrast, large *couture* houses like Chanel and Saint Laurent employ more than a hundred staff in one or a combination of several *ateliers* which are separated into *flou* for dressmaking and *tailleur* for the tailoring of suits and coats. In the larger houses, *modelistes*, who work under the head designers, liaise with the *atelier* and oversee the construction of the *toile* (sample garment). Each atelier is headed by the *premier d'atelier* or production manager who oversees the workforce of *vendeuses* (sales assistants), fitters, *midinettes* (seamstresses who are usually divided into first and second hands) and apprentices.

The third criterion for *couture* classification requires that the clothes be entirely made-to-measure – there must be no partial cutting of fabrics or assembling of parts before the client has been measured. Further conditions insist that *couturiers* show their collections twice a year – in the last week of January and the last week of July – and that there must be a minimum of 65 garments each season. This stipulation effectively bars many new or financially unstable houses from gaining official *Chambre Syndicale* classification, the holders of which are entitled to free exposure on state-run television as well as

Craftsmen at work in the *atelier* of the House of Hermes.

John Galliano became the first British designer to take over a French *couture* house at Givenchy. He now heads Dior.

government payment for shows of *couture* world-wide. The cost of producing a single *couture* collection – in the region of $1 million (c. £613,500) – is substantially offset by such free advertising, and by export sales which are currently in the region of 55 per cent of everything French *couture* houses produce.

It is estimated that there are fewer than a thousand women world-wide who can afford to buy a *couture* dress, which can cost anything between $5,000 and $50,000 (c.£3000-£35,000). However, *couture* remains the prestigious showpiece of French fashion and the place for creativity and originality in design.

The undoubted master of *couture* is Yves Saint Laurent, who at the age of 17 began his career as assistant to Christian Dior and opened his own business in 1962. One of the most recent coups has been scored by John Galliano: his appointment to succeed Hubert de Givenchy as head of the House of Givenchy in Paris made Galliano the first British designer ever to take over a French *couture* house. He has since replaced Gianfranco Ferre at Christian Dior.

Other *couturiers* include Emmanuel Ungaro, who spent four years with Balenciaga and a year with Courrèges before opening his own salon in 1965, and Claude Montana, who was chosen to design *couture* for the oldest house in Paris, the House of Lanvin, in 1989. In houses where the original *couturier* is no longer living, others have taken over the responsibility for *couture* while a second designer is employed for the *prêt-à-porter* line. Examples include Michel Goma for Balenciaga, Erik Mortensen for Pierre Balmain, Angelo Tarlazzi at Guy Laroche and Gerard Pipart for Nina Ricci.

THE EMPIRE BUILDERS

In contrast to the anonymity of the early *couturiers*, today's designers appear on the covers of magazines and in advertisements for their own products, products that are considered symbols of excellence and beauty by both the rich and famous and the ordinary man or woman in the street. Furthermore fashion is truly international: Karl Lagerfeld designs *couture* for Chanel and furs for Fendi of Italy; his own less expensive KL line is German. Nicole Farhi, who is French,

designs in London while American Richard Tyler designs in Italy for Byblos. Paradoxically while the profits from *couture* continue to decline, as was evidenced by the declassification of Courrèges when the house failed to show *couture* collections for two consecutive seasons, the designer is in the ascendant. In France, North America, Britain, Italy and Japan and, more recently, in Germany, Spain, Belgium and the Netherlands, designers have achieved international celebrity, and the most successful international designers are superstars.

Today, however, a successful business is not built solely on a good designer. Behind all the leading designers is an astute business mind: at Saint Laurent, Pierre Bergé's takeover of Charles of the Ritz made Yves Saint Laurent the only living *couturier* to own his own perfume house. Bergé's negotiations reputedly net $1 million (c.£613,500) from tobacco giant R.J. Reynolds, who manufacture the stubs for Saint Laurent's designer cigarettes. Since 1960, Giancarlo Giametti has supervised the Valentino empire which employs over 6,000 people and produces 90 collections per year. At Ralph Lauren, Peter Strom successfully switched the company's activities almost entirely into licensing deals whereby the manufacturer finances the production, shipping and part of the promotional costs thus freeing Lauren (and himself) from the risks and costs of actually making clothes. Other companies have been bought by financiers to create luxury goods conglomerates: Bernard Arnault, president of the powerful Financière Agache, a textile

Designer Yves Saint Laurent (left) and Pierre Bergé (right), the business brain behind the fashion empire.

conglomerate which owns Boussac, Christian Dior, Givenchy and the luxury leather goods manufacturer Louis Vuitton, was also financial backer of Christian Lacroix when he left the House of Patou in 1987.

Today's successful designer is a business person who is personally involved not only in design but also in production, sales, public relations and advertising. The development of the fashion industry is evident in both its growth in revenue and the increasingly wide range of products being marketed by designers – from perfumes, bedlinens and sunglasses to lingerie, stationery and luggage. American designer Oscar de la Renta reputedly turns over more than $500 (c. £310) million worth of products world-wide, has 45 licencees and three perfumes, while Ralph Lauren exemplifies the diversity of a contemporary fashion designer's work: in addition to womenswear, there are the

Ralph Lauren launches a new line of clothing from a truck at New York University.

fragrances, the home furnishings and, of course, menswear. Lauren is a good example of a designer who has built an empire on lifestyle. In 1986, *Time* magazine priced the Ralph Lauren empire at $1.3 billion and estimated Lauren's personal fortune at something in the region of $300 (c. £190) million. Lauren receives 5–8 per cent of wholesale revenues or approximately $20 (c. £12) million per year from his licensing business. Lauren's four most important licensees are Sosmaire Inc. which manufactures Lauren's

fragrances; Ralph Lauren Womenswear Inc. (manufactured by the giant Bidermann Industries USA division); Chaps by Ralph Lauren (lower-priced suits manufactured by Greif Cos., lower-priced ties and shirts made by the C.F. Hathaway Group) and Ralph Lauren Home Furnishings Inc. (bedlinens manufactured by J.P. Stevens).

The king of licensing remains Pierre Cardin whose approximately 800 licensees include fruit juices, canned fish and wet suits. With an estimated personal income of around $10 (c. £6) million per year, Cardin's name is linked to more than 500 factories world-wide; in addition he owns the restaurant chain Maxim's, the latest of which opened in 1996 in Moscow.

Over the past 20 years, fashion designers like Ralph Lauren, Giorgio Armani and Calvin Klein have created empires, their boutiques acting as embassies in all the major capital cities of the world. As with monarchs, it is their very image whch sustains loyalty: in Italy, Armani, Versace and Mariuccia Mandelli, who owns Krizia with her husband Aldo Pinto, are frequently the subjects of the gossip columns. For Italian designers the most important personal and

publicity asset is the *palazzo*: the headquarters of Giorgio Armani is located in a seventeenth-century *palazzo* in Milan where he produces 500 designs for each collection. Staff in Armani's design studio are employed only to turn his sketches into patterns, a feature that is almost unique to Armani.

In France, Karl Lagerfeld, dubbed the Napoleon of *couture*, spends most of his time at his chateau in Brittany, yet still manages to be photographed frequently at parties and nightclubs. But of all the designers who have successfully marketed themselves alongside their clothes, Calvin Klein is the undisputed leader.

'The undisputed king of licensing' Pierre Cardin outside the Maxim restaurant in Paris.

Calvin Klein

Born the son of a grocer in the Bronx in 1942, Calvin Klein graduated from the New York Fashion Institute of Technology. A succession of low-paid jobs in the garment industry followed before he borrowed $10,000 (c. £6250) from his old friend and now business partner, Barry Schwartz. What Klein realized was that in order to sell clothes in their millions he had to offer something else than just garments. The 'something else' in Klein's hands was 'attitude' and 'lifestyle', and his clothes, simply cut and in plain colours, could be worn anywhere by almost anyone. In 1978, Klein spent $5 (c. £3) million on the sexually overt jeans advertisements 'Nothing comes between me and my Calvins' starring teen model Brooke Shields. While American designers were usually somewhat anonymous, Klein appeared in his own advertising, and through the gossip columns began to acquire the status and glamour of a rock star. Even his apartment shared in this position when it was loaned out

for the making of *Superman*. Yet there was a price to pay: his first marriage ended in divorce and in 1978 his daughter Marci was kidnapped on her way home from school. She was released after Klein dropped the ransom of $100,000 (c. £62,500) at a pick-up point in the Pan American Building in New York City. In 1986, Klein reinvented himself following his marriage to Kelly Rector, an assistant in his design studio, and again his advertising reflected his new persona. In 1985, his perfume Obsession had been promoted by blue-lit ads depicting three naked figures of indeterminate sex together on a sofa. By 1988 his change in lifestyle, including his treatment for drink and drug addiction, was mirrored by the advertising for his next perfume, Eternity. Clearly Klein's priorities – at least where the Calvin Klein image is concerned – have substantially changed since the wild partying of the pre-AIDS years. He has reinvented himself as 'Calvin Clean', the archetypal caring, sharing, healthy and happy persona of the 1990s.

One of America's most successful international designers, Calvin Klein with his wife Kelly. A leading player in the designer jeans and perfumes fields, Klein has instigated advertising campaigns that reflect the changing attitudes and lifestyles of the last decades of the twentieth century.

THE FASHION MEDIA

Today, fashion is big news and the mass media covers the stories in both editorial copy and paid advertisement messages. The fashion press, whether glossy magazines, the fashion sections of the daily newspapers, specialist publications like *Women's Wear Daily* or television programmes like the BBC's *Clothes Show*, is a crucial link between the fashion industry and the consumer and one which the designer must exploit.

Fashion magazines, which for the most part report on and interpret fashion news for the consumer, have been around for more than 150 years. In America, *Godey's Lady's Book* which began publication in 1831, gave advice on fabrics, showed pictures of the latest fashions and, of course, carried advertisements. Its male counterpart was *Burton's Gentleman's Magazine* which was edited from 1839 to 1840 by the American Gothic novelist Edgar Allan Poe. In England, *The Englishwoman's Domestic Magazine* (founded 1853) and *The Queen* (1861) were owned by Samuel Beeton, publisher of his wife's famous cookery book.

The increased interest in fashion was catered for by the rise in women's magazines and in the 1930s, mass circulation really took off. *Woman's Own* was founded in 1932 and *Woman*, launched in 1937, had nearly half a million readers by the end of its first year of publication. But it was the 1950s that saw the heyday of magazines when the readership of *Woman*, *Woman's Own* and *Women's Realm* ran into millions. *Vogue* remained universally popular and extended its service to 'home sewers' with the Vogue Pattern Service which negotiated contracts with a number of leading *couturiers* including Balmain, Fath, Schiaparelli, Lanvin, Molyneux and Paquin to make available to readers accurate paper patterns for even the most complicated of *couture* dresses.

MEN'S FASHION PUBLISHING

The 1980s saw the advent of a sustained effort by designers to capitalize on the male market. The rise of men's ready-to-wear and of male fashion consumers was catered to by the growth of men's fashion and style magazines such as *Vogue Men*, *Cosmo Man*, *The Face*, *I-D*, *GQ* and *Arena*, while other magazines, including the colour supplements of Sunday

THE FASHIONS Expressly designed and prepared for the Englishwoman's Domestic Magazine.

DECEMBER 1860

The Englishwoman's Domestic Magazine was founded in 1853 by Samuel Beeton.

newspapers, began to incorporate special fashion and style sections for men. In an attempt to appeal to the 'new man', designers' advertising played on traditional ideas of masculinity – competitiveness, 'friendly' aggression and notions of rugged individuality – in order to nudge men into the non-traditional role of fashion consumer. Not only did the magazines promote men's clothing but they also featured entire new ranges of 'fashion' products including skin and hair care for the contemporary, fashionable man. Even the daily routine of shaving was now a part of a glamorous lifestyle, something that square-jawed airline pilots and athletes did each day to maintain their rugged good looks and the attention of their women.

Designers have found print, particularly the glossy, full colour magazines, the most effective fashion-advertising medium. Furthermore, they have realized that their adverts no longer need to be restricted exclusively to either men's or women's magazines; fashion advertising (which for the main part is 'brand-name reinforcement' advertising) appears to be equally effective in both. Today's magazines have a high dual-readership number: both men and women read *Arena* and *GQ* and men's style magazines are bought by women for their male partners.

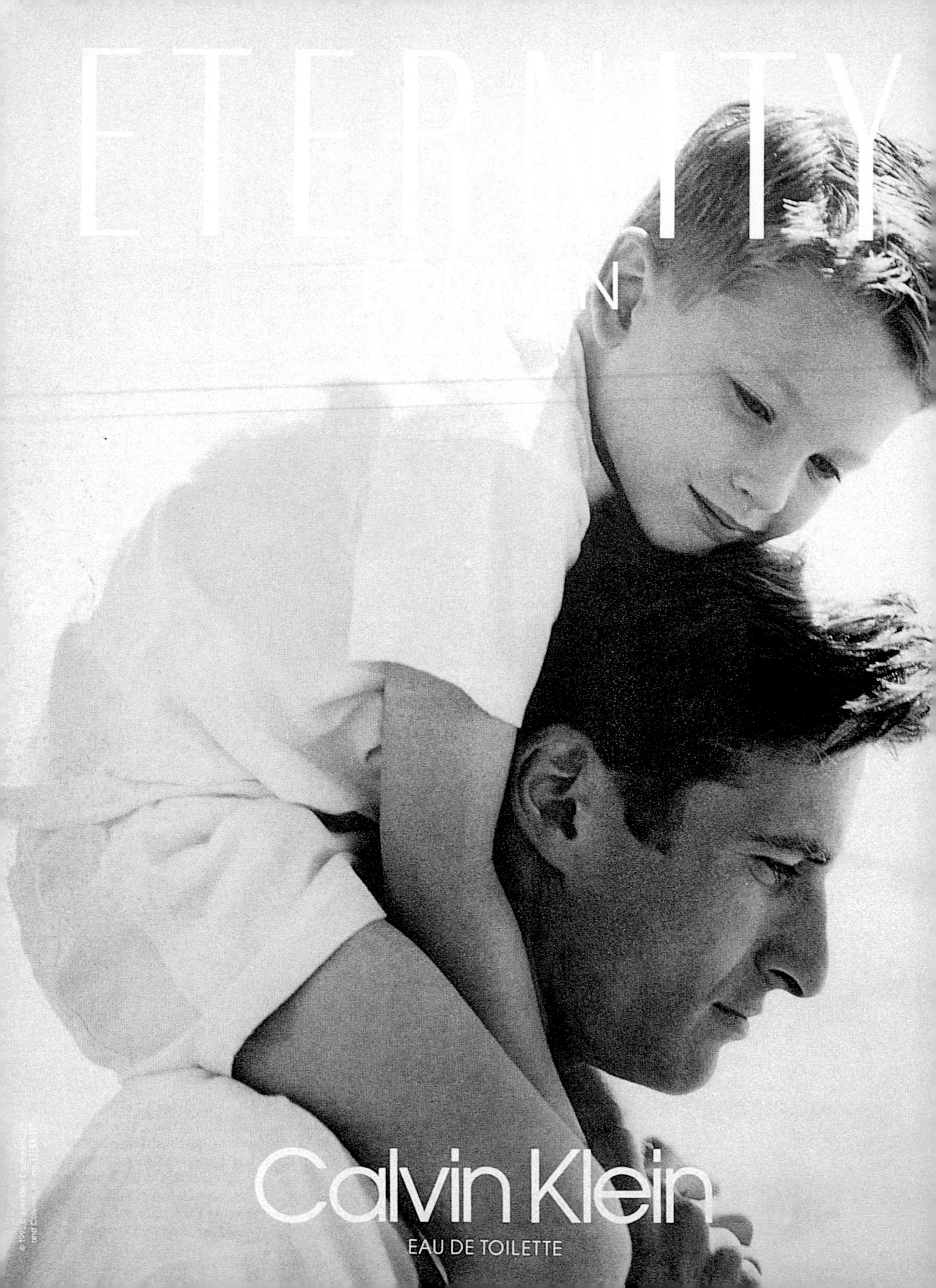
ETERNITY
Calvin Klein
EAU DE TOILETTE

Left: Calvin Klein: Eternity for Men. One of the products targeted at the lucrative male market as designers, already successful with womenswear and women's merchandising, sought to extend their ranges.

However, there remains a certain sense of homophobia associated with the idea of men looking at pictures of other physically attractive men. Consequently, men's style magazines are filled with images of beautiful, fashionably dressed (and undressed) women who accompany (some might argue 'accessorize') the male models.

THE INFLUENCE OF FASHION MAGAZINES

The role fashion magazines play is a complex one: they act as reporters on the global fashion scene, reflecting, featuring and promoting styles they consider newsworthy. One of the most powerful women in fashion publishing is Anna Wintour, reputedly nicknamed 'Nuclear Wintour', editor-in-chief of *American Vogue*: at fashion shows it is directly in front of her seat that the models stop and hold a pose.

Sometimes the magazines influence fashion, especially when editors take an active part in the creation of merchandise they consider acceptable to their audience: *Elle* magazine regularly features a garment specially created for its readers. At the same time, magazines are part of the distribution of fashion, encouraging retailers to stock the merchandise they have featured in their pages. Finally, the magazines also provide

Above: Anna Wintour, one of the most powerful women in the fashion publishing world. It is directly in front of her seat at fashion shows that designers instruct their models to stop and pose!

information to consumers about approximate prices, designers and retailers.

An important weapon in the magazine's style armoury is the 'editorial credit'. Once

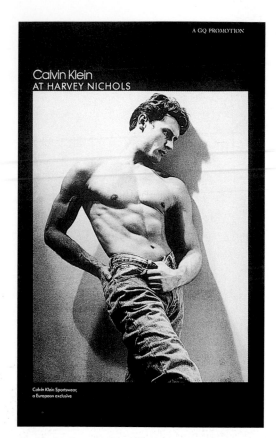

Above: Designer, retailer and magazine join forces: Calvin Klein menswear available at speciality store Harvey Nichols in London, as advertised in *GQ*.

the fashion editors have made their selections, the garments and accessories that in their opinion are the fashion statements of the season are photographed and appear in their pages alongside the names of the designers or manufacturers, the name of at least one retail store where the items can be bought and their approximate prices. The 'endorsement' of merchandise by the magazine editorial encourages manufacturers to make garments in enough numbers, retailers to stock them and customers to buy them. Hang tags or 'As seen in' in-store advertising boards remind consumers that this is the garment he or she has read about.

Advertising in fashion magazines

As with most publications, the fashion magazines' principal revenue is derived from the sale of advertising space. In fact, advertising can account for as much as 50 per cent of the total number of pages in a fashion magazine. This dependency on income from advertisers, such as the designers, rather than from sales of the magazine does not always lead to impartial fashion reporting. In Italy a system of trading off editorial photographs with pages of advertising has been established. If an Italian designer books advertising in an Italian magazine, he or she 'naturally' expects to see their clothes featured also in the fashion stories. This practice, increasingly copied throughout Europe and North America, is a useful tactic for designers as they can predict more accurately the amount of press exposure their collections can expect. Furthermore, because the editorial pages are perceived by readers to have more authority or to be more 'credible' than the pages devoted to advertising, this type of publicity is all the more desirable for the designer.

Right: Chanel advertisement. Most of a magazine's revenue is derived from the sale of advertising space. Brand leader designers spend millions of dollars a year reinforcing their names with the consumer, encouraging them to buy into the 'designer' lifestyle.

CHANEL

Related to the designer's intense marketing of their fashions is the development of free, glossy, magazines which are supported entirely by advertising revenue. One of the earliest, launched in 1981, was *Portrait* which was distributed to 100,000 'high-value' properties in London, and promoted exclusive designer lifestyles in both its editorial and advertising. The bubble burst for *Portrait* and many magazines like it when the boom years of the 1980s ended. Falling stock market prices and rising mortgage rates meant that many of those 100,000 high-value homeowners found themselves in the negative equity trap.

Fashion magazine editors are constantly walking a tightrope between fair and accurate fashion reporting and the need to generate income for their publishers through carrying the advertisements of specific designers. Furthermore, they are often viewed by the public as arbiters of taste, negotiating the changing roles and images of women, new fashion and style, the demands of the designers and the public's notions of 'acceptable good taste'. Both the fashion designer and the fashion consumer, not surprisingly, have a love–hate relationship with fashion editors and their journals.

Fashion magazines are often condemned for encouraging conspicuous consumption and 'throw-away' attitudes in a time when the world's resources cannot necessarily be renewed; likewise, for their reinforcement of gender, class, racial and physical stereotypes through their use of young, predominantly white and skinny female models, which emphasizes this perception. The magazines are even blamed for encouraging in teenage girls every psychological disorder from disenchantment with the shape of their breasts or noses to the eating disorders anorexia nervosa and bulimia.

THE POWER OF THE PRESS

Designers have millions of dollars worth of orders riding on the success of their catwalk shows and the reception of the press and buyers to their latest offerings. The fashion designers – whose economic life depends on getting their clothes featured and endorsed in the magazines' editorials – can be quick to turn their venom on fashion editors. The *Evening Standard*'s Lowri Turner was banned from attending Gianni Versace's and Christian Lacroix's shows when she was less than complimentary in her reviews of their collections; Carrie Donavon was excluded from Valentino's shows after she likened his *couture* customers to 'china dolls', and even John Fairchild, chairman and chief executive of Fairchild Publications was banned at Yves Saint Laurent after his journals championed Lacroix's first collection. The battle raged on as Fairchild banned all coverage of YSL in the pages of the Fairchild press empire while Saint Laurent himself ordered the cancellation of the company's not insubstantial advertising accounts in Fairchild's press.

Women's Wear Daily

The difference between the fashion magazines like *Vogue*, *Elle* or *Harper's Bazaar*, and Fairchild's publications like *W* and *Women's Wear Daily*, is that the former are aimed at the consumer, featuring current fashions that are already available in retail stores while Fairchild's publications are trade papers. *Women's Wear Daily* is published five times a week and covers the 'fashion waterfront' – the raw materials, the manufacturing and retailing of fashion, as well as keeping a watchful eye on the wardrobes of the rich and famous and the trend-setters. To most people in the fashion industry, *WWD* is the fashion bible.

Founded in 1890 by E.W. Fairchild, *WWD* has its headquarters in New York City but maintains offices throughout the United States, Europe and Asia and reports on the collections, the fashion events, and the personnel changes in fashion companies at executive level. *WWD* also often produces special supplements devoted to subjects such as accessories or new technological developments in fibres or manufacturing processes. *W* is a bi-monthly, condensed version of *WWD* that is produced in colour. Each year, *W* publishes its infamous IN and OUT lists – reputedly compiled by John Fairchild himself – as well as 'The World's Top Fifty Designers' supplement. To appear in the OUT list or to be excluded from the Top Fifty is the fashion industry's equivalent of leprosy.

TELEVISION AND FASHION

While magazines and newspapers are still regarded by designers as the most effective vehicles for promoting and advertising fashion and fashion-related goods, increasingly they have been harnessing the power of television. Not only do viewers see the advertisements of manufacturers and retailers of fashion, but they also see contemporary fashions in the entertainment programmes. Unfortunately, due to the short life-span of fashion apparel, advertising designer clothing on television is a difficult and expensive task. Television commercials are therefore primarily used for reinforcing brand recognition of a designer's name and for volume-selling those related items such as perfumes and cosmetics that carry the designer name. However, in the late 1970s, and coinciding with the rise of designer ready-to-wear and the recognition of the immense selling power of designer names, the 'designer jeans wars', with Gloria Vanderbilt, Jordache and Calvin Klein amongst the combatants, were fought out on the battleground of television.

In 1979, Calvin Klein followed up his previous year's successful poster campaign, which reputedly cost $5 (c. £3) million and starred the 15-year-old actress and model Brooke Shields, with the $16 (c. £10) million series of television commercials 'Nothing Comes Between Me and My Calvins', again starring Ms Shields in a variety of provocative poses. The sensuous visuals – criticized by many observers as overtly sexual and

Teen-model and actress Brooke Shields in the campaign for Calvin Klein's signature jeans in 1979. The ads caused sensation but encouraged a 300% increase in the sales of Calvin Klein jeans.

salacious, particularly when they featured such a young girl – caused controversy and sensation. None the less, the adverts encouraged a 300 per cent increase in the sale of Calvin Klein jeans.

Klein is no stranger to controversial advertising: in the US, his underwear advertisements featuring Bruce Weber's erotic photographs of bronzed, well-toned young male models clad only in the designer's products, caused a near scandal but nevertheless initiated the current trend of 'male-as-sex-object' advertising both in the press and on television. This tendency has been exploited most fully by Levi's who in their British television commercial had Nick Kamen strip to his underpants in a launderette.

Today's advertising knows no bounds and appears almost everywhere: brand names and designer logos like DKNY and CK appear on huge billboards in city centres, on t-shirts, shopping bags and even across the front of our shoes if they're not already embossed on the soles. Free gifts of tote bags, umbrellas, dressing gowns and product samples have become effective marketing devices for designers promoting consumer awareness of new products, reinforcing brand identity and encouraging consumer loyalty, as well as becoming sought-after 'collectables' by the true fashion victim.

Contemporary advertising is now a legitimate art form, with prizes for excellence and museums devoting display space to it. Advertising now even sells itself in the form of poster and postcard reproductions. One thing fashion shares with the advertising industry is the key tactic of surprise. Like fashion, advertising has to maintain novelty, to keep creating new images and to attract customer's attention to what are often the most mundane of objects. French fashion retailers Kookai are famous for their unorthodox advertising campaigns, for example, Linda Evangelista exhorting mothers not to let their daughters wear Kookai clothes. Kookai became the first women's clothes store to be promoted by male models: in the campaign that broke in April 1996 – 'Stop staring. It's only a Kookai girl', Matthew, Nathan, James Neal and Jamie Spear from Select Models proved a big hit with both the teenage shopper and her mother. Where once avant-garde art used to cause outrage, now it is fashion and its advertised images which seek to be new and creative. When Calvin Klein launched his range of tailored underpants as modelled by Tim Hinthams, 'fans' (both of Hinthams in particular and of young attractive men dressed only in their underpants in general) smashed the glass in hundreds of New York bus shelters to steal the posters.

Yet, because we are so familiar with advertising we are, in fact, no longer convinced by it. But we still expect to be entertained by advertising and we still like to be seduced by it. Consequently, designers continue to use the most classic weapon of seduction – beauty. When companies like Benetton deviate too far from the accepted norms of beauty and fashion advertising, public outrage ensues.

To maintain their share of the market, brand leaders like Giorgio Armani, Chanel, Calvin Klein, Christian Dior and Donna Karan must spend millions of dollars world-wide on advertising their names. But no amount of spending can ever guarantee a successful product, no matter how famous your name is. When Christian Lacroix launched his signature perfume 'C'est La Vie', the advertising campaign cost in excess of $40 (c. £25) million. Despite heavy print and television advertising, the perfume did not have that sweet smell of success and was a flop with the consumer. But, as the French would probably say with a Gallic shrug of their shoulders, 'C'est la vie' or rather, 'C'est la mode'.

To maintain their share of the market, designers must spend millions on advertising their names.

GIORGIO ARMANI
PARFUMS

CORPORATE FACES

Although *haute couture* properly came into being in the mid-nineteenth century, it was not until the beginning of the twentieth century that it adopted the rhythm of creation and presentation that is familiar to us today. In the beginning, there were no collections to be presented at fixed dates – new models were created throughout the year and varied only according to the season. Nor were there organized fashion shows: these really began around 1908 and later developed into more aesthetic spectacles presented at fixed hours in the afternoon in the great fashion houses' salons.

THE FASHION SHOW

After World War I, as professional buyers sought out more model outfits, the seasonal show began to be organized on more or less fixed dates. From then on, in late January and July, every great Paris *couture* house presented its summer and winter collections. Later, in response to pressure from foreign buyers, autumn (fall) and spring (or half-season) collections were presented in April and October. These collections were first shown to foreign buyers – especially Americans – while private clients were admitted two or three weeks later.

As *haute couture* established itself, fashion presentation became institutionalized and orchestrated, occurring for the most part twice a year, since the half-season collections really offered little more than a hint of fashions to come. But, importantly, the use of live models and the advent of the catwalk or runway show removed the traditional relationship between 'dressmaker' and client and replaced it with a system that gave increasing autonomy in matters of taste, style and fashion to the designer-*couturiers*. When models wore outfits that clients only had to choose from, customers lost the initiative in matters of dress. At most, all the elegant client could do now was introduce very minor modifications, but even these would be done under the watchful eye of the house *vendeuses* who would ensure that the spirit of the

On the catwalk at Versace (1997). The model has become one of a designer's most powerful marketing tools – and one of the most expensive items in the fashion show budget.

collection and its trademark look were not distilled beyond recognition.

With the advent of ready-to-wear, the once hushed and reverently-staged ceremonial processions of *haute couture* outfits worn by the *cabine* (the *couturier*'s private group of house models) gave way to expensive, theatrically-produced sound-and-light shows with internationally-known models as performers, and sometimes, actual performers, for instance, when members of Stuttgart Ballet appeared as models for Issey Miyake.

In 1975, fourteen top Italian designers which had previously held their shows in Florence, broke ranks and headed for Milan to mount their twice-yearly ready-to-wear shows in March and October. Paris followed suit and by the late 1970s, the European runway shows had blossomed into today's costly staged productions starring the world's supermodels.

On the catwalk

The fashion runways now stalked by today's catwalk kittens came into being at a trade fair held in Chicago in 1914. This marked the first use of a specially constructed catwalk that projected into the audience in order to give a good view of the clothes. Runway shows were originally devised to sell clothes. Today, however, most buying is in fact done pre-show. The runway show exists to give buyers an opportunity to reopen their order books and add to their purchases and to encourage new buyers to place orders. For the designer, the major role of the show is, increasingly, as a

The more experienced the photographer and the more prestigious the client the better the shooting position, but each is expected to get the photograph of the outfit of the collection worn by the model of the show!

crucial part of the publicity machine.

Haute couture runway shows are essentially promotional devices giving a brand name for advertising high-fashion ready-to-wear and other items sold under its label world-wide. The *haute couture* presentations no longer exist to dress women in the latest fashions but instead keep alive the traditions of luxury and virtuosity in design by showing masterpieces of workmanship that often pay no heed to practical or commercial obligations. The successful runway show means photographs, and photographs generate sales and promote the designer's name which is in turn used to endorse items from the extended line of perfumes, hosiery, sunglasses and other accessories.

The international ready-to-wear designer shows have remained exclusive to all but the élite: only a thousand people are invited to occupy around six hundred seats. But this very exclusivity has created such media interest that the latest looks can now be seen by all on television and in the pages of magazines and newspapers. The catwalk show today has become a form of entertainment, a fact recognized by many retailers and broadcasters who have organized in-store catwalk shows and major public events like the BBC's *Clothes Show Live* exhibitions. Meanwhile, designers

Such is the celebrity of some designers, like Paloma Picasso, their own image will advertise their merchandise.

Backstage at Tommy Hilfiger.

who recognize the power of their own celebrity, for example Paloma Picasso, either appear in advertisements for their own products or take to the road at home and abroad on trunk shows, travelling with their ready-to-wear collections that are shown in-store to customers unable or unwilling to travel to the European, New York or Tokyo shows. In trunk shows, designers and their collections come to the customers, who are offered the opportunity to see every item in the line and to order through the store any styles, colours or sizes that have not been stocked. Trunk shows provide the designer with first-hand experience of consumers' reaction to the collection, while retailers can see consumer response to what their buyers – rightly or wrongly – did or did not select.

Runway shows come in all shapes and sizes, from the annual end-of-year shows by fashion students to intimate shows in salons where the guests are seated on gilded chairs. Recently, designers have employed all manner of shock tactics from nudity and cross-dressing to the use of celebrities as models in order to generate or guarantee public and media interest. A dress is front-page news if, like Yves Saint Laurent, you have extracts from the Koran embroidered on it and manage to offend millions of Moslems for whom the text is sacred. The dress was subsequently removed from the collection but not before the whole world came to know of it.

Equalling the media hype surrounding the designer catwalk shows is the amount of money spent on producing them. It is estimated that a Paris designer's ready-to-wear show costs something in the region of $200,000 (c. £125,000) to stage. A typical show will include photography (house photography and video/film recording) at around $40,000 (c. £25,000), invitations costing around $5,000 (c. £3125), music and lights at $5,000 (c. £3125), hairdressing at $10,000 (c. £6250), sets and catwalk construction at $20,000 (c. £12,500), ushers and security (for the clothes) cost another $6,500 (c. £4050); venue hire – often an exhibition tent – at $38,000 (c. £23,750) and press dossiers at $10,000 (c. £6250). Add to this the cost of accessories' hire, the designer perfumes given to selected guests and members of the press, the cost of fitters for the models, pressers for the clothes, stylists, make-up artists, champagne refreshments, PR, travel and accommodation.

And it's all over in about 40 minutes.

A BRIEF HISTORY OF THE MODEL

The most expensive items that grace the designer shows today are what Michael Gross of *New York* magazine has called 'genetic accidents': the new pin-ups of the modern generation, the models who since the 1980s have become the most powerful marketing tool in the fashion industry and play their part in the theatricalization of merchandise, the appeal to desire and the artful, even fanciful advertising of fashion in all its manifestations.

Naomi, Kate, Christy, Claudia, Helena, Cindy, Linda: we are on first-name terms with them. They are the icons of our society, metaphors for both commerce and culture. The supermodels are the visual projection of the dreams of millions who copy their looks; they represent the contemporary canons of beauty and glamour and are as celebrated as the movie and rock stars they date. The supermodels have come a long way from the silent and often anonymous *cabine* mannequins of the early part of this century, who had little social standing and were often considered disreputable women, just one step above actresses.

The first recorded instance of models selling fashion actually involved wooden dolls dressed in miniature versions of *couture* clothes. The dolls were sent to wealthy clients

Texan-born Bridget Hall has all the physical pre-requisites of a successful model.

in the capitals of Europe in the seventeenth century, and later to the Americas. By the mid-eighteenth century, the first fashion magazine had appeared displaying the works of the first named *couturier*, Rose Bertin, the official *couturier* at the Court of Versailles. The concept of using live models for showing clothes grew out of the *couture* industry. *Demoiselles des magasins* as they were called were in use from the 1860s and were young women employed by salons and stores to display the latest styles to regular customers. Marie Vernet is credited with being the first professional model: following her marriage in 1852 to English-born *couturier* Charles Worth, Marie extended the role of the 'house model' outside the salon and became a sort of walking advertisement for her husband's creations. Since then, many designers have had their 'model-muses': Paul Poiret and his wife Denise; John Galliano and Lady Harlech; Karl Lagerfeld and Ines de la Fressange and now Claudia Schiffer; Yves Saint Laurent and Loulou de la Falaise Klossowski; Donna Karan and her 'alter-ego' Rosemary MacRother.

The first photographic model of repute was the Countess de Castiglione, a Tuscan noblewoman at the court of Napoleon III. In 1856 a book of 288 photographs by Adolphe Braun displayed the countess's style and wardrobe; in some pictures she even daringly lifted the hems of her skirts to reveal her shoes. For many years, photographic models continued to be socialites, actresses and dancers. Today the distinction between a runway model and a photographic model still remains: runway models can be larger and taller than photographic models since the camera tends to distort size and is suited to smaller models. However, since the 1980s, many have been doing both kinds of work.

Modelling started to gain recognition as a profession in Britain and America in the late 1920s with the establishment of model agencies like Lucie Clayton's in 1928. Around the same time Paul Poiret began to take his models on early 'trunk shows', first to fashionable venues like the races at Longchamps and later to other European capitals. The greatest boost to modelling came from Jean Patou, the first designer to put his own initials on the outside of the garments he designed. Recognizing the potential of the American market Patou decided to recruit American models and he held the first 'model search'. Considerable publicity surrounded the event and was enough to encourage 400 hopeful models to turn up to audition. Patou selected six new faces and thereby launched modelling as a new industry.

Surprisingly, in France, the heart of the fashion world, it would not be until the 1950s that modelling was professionalized, in part because there were no model agencies. In France, employment agencies had been banned since it was considered illegal for

Model muses: once it was Ines de la Fressange, now it is Claudia Schiffer (right) who inspires Karl Lagerfeld (left).

anyone to take a percentage of someone else's income; such an arrangement mirrored that of pimps and prostitutes, and so models in Paris made their own bookings. In the mid-1950s, model Dorien Leigh, the first in a long line of 'faces' for Revlon which had begun its 'Fire and Ice' advertising campaign in 1952, emigrated to France and circumvented the country's employment laws by opening a model agency which took fees from clients and not the models. In the 1950s, mannequins, as they were still called, started to become media personalities and some even married into the aristocracy: Fiona Campbell Walter married Baron von Thyssen, one of the richest men in Europe; Jane MacNeil married the Earl of Dalkeith and Bronwen Pugh married Lord Astor. Other models like Bettina Graziano, one of Paris's top models, who worked exclusively for Givenchy in the 1950s, had a blouse named after her. By the 1960s, individual models – Twiggy, who later went on to a successful career as an actress, Jean Shrimpton and Verushka – had become household names and international celebrities.

MODEL INTO SUPERMODEL

By the 1970s, models evolved into superstars. This trend has continued, and the models' changing status has been reflected in their earning potential. In the 1940s, American models earned about $25 (c. £15) a day. By the 1970s, a top model could demand around $5000 (c. £3125) a day. Today the supermodels are reputed to earn between $10,000 and $15,000 per show (c. £6000-£10,000). In 1995, supermodel Claudia Schiffer was the world's highest earning model, reputedly grossing around $12 (c. £7.5) million a year. Supermodels are no longer naive adolescents but career professionals, businesswomen able to negotiate the conditions of their complex contracts to ensure that their names and their faces remain hot property long after their catwalk days are over and they turn to product endorsement or careers as television presenters and actresses.

Increasingly, designers have demanded older models for their campaigns: Levi's latest print adverts use septuagenarian models who also happen to be 'real people'; Lisa Taylor at 40 years old was rehired by Calvin Klein after she criticized his policy of having young models promoting fashions aimed at older women.

In 1973 Lauren Hutton, then aged 32, made history when she signed the first exclusive modelling contract in the cosmetics business, agreeing to pose only for Revlon's Ultima brand in exchange for $400,000 (c. £250,000) over two years. Hutton's association with Revlon ended in 1984, but by this stage she had made the transformation from model to actress with film appearances in *Paper Lion*, *Welcome to LA* and *American Gigolo*. Hutton's modelling career was far from over however: 'rediscovered' in the late 1980s by Mark McCormack's International Management Group (IMG), at the age of 50, Hutton for the second time in her career became a Revlon girl and the face of fashion manufacturer and retailers Hennes, as well as returning to the catwalk for American designers, including Calvin Klein.

Others, however, have not been so lucky: Lançome recently dropped their corporate model Isabella Rossellini claiming she was too old. IMG also recently announced that it was dispensing with contracts of several models who they considered were no longer in their prime. It's not surprising then that many supermodels today – most of whom are already in their thirties – have turned to pop singing or novels (Naomi Campbell), exercise videos (Cindy Crawford and Elle 'The Body' MacPherson) and television presenting (Cindy Crawford and Tyra Banks).

As the models' status has changed over

the years so too have their relationships with the designers: Poiret would demand that his customers ignored the *cabine* models saying that they 'were not there'; designer and photographer Cecil Beaton called models 'silly cows' behind their backs, while Christian Dior preferred to find his models in the brothels of Cannes, Deauville and Monte Carlo. Coco Chanel preferred her models to be dark-haired and look very much like herself. She also consistently refused to raise their salaries, commenting that they could live off their looks by getting a rich lover to support them.

Once at the beck and call of agents, photographers and designers, models today are tough negotiators: Cindy Crawford turned down top photographer Bruce Weber's request that she pose nude for Calvin Klein hosiery and perfume, not because she would be nude, but because her face wouldn't be seen. When the European designers complained that supermodels' fees were excessive and boycotted them, they soon realized they had lost an international sales tool and begged them to return. Attracting top models to show at collection time has now become one of a fashion designer's top priorities.

Sound businesswomen supermodels need to be, particularly when it comes to exclusive contracts with designers, manufacturers or cosmetic companies. While an exclusive contract guarantees income and has brought fame to many models – Cindy Crawford for Revlon, Pauline Poriskova for Estée Lauder, Claudia Schiffer for Guess?, Stephanie Seymour for L'Oréal, Christy Turlington for Maybelline and Carol Bouquet, the corporate face of Chanel, whose contract demands her attendance at each season's runway shows – the contracts can be watertight. In addition to undertaking all areas of broadcast advertising and promotion, from TV and magazines to packaging, display materials and retail store trunk shows, Jose Borain's contract for Calvin Klein's Obsession specified that she maintain the same weight, the same hair style and colour and precise body appearance throughout her contract. Other contracts include 'morality clauses' that specify that models' lifestyles are appropriate to trademarks they are promoting.

Once anonymous clothes-horses, now models are synonymous with fashion itself. With the constant shifting of power relationships within the fashion industry, we may soon see the day when the models are better known than the designers whose clothes they model.

Cindy Crawford: the corporate face of Revlon. An exclusive contract identifies the model's beauty with the designer's products.

MASCARA CAN MAKE
LASHES LOOK THICKER
ON THE OUTSIDE

INNER LASH

ALSO MAKES
LASHES THICKER
FROM THE INSIDE.

It's a mascara breakthrough.
Inner Lash penetrates each
individual lash to thicken,
condition and protect lashes
from the inside out. High
density colour separates,
thickens and lengthens. Leaves
lashes soft and supple. Now
your lashes really stand out.

DRESSING SOCIETY

For many people, the role of the fashion designer is synonymous with 'fashion leadership', since there is the widespread belief that it is solely designers who originate new styles, some of which become fashion trends. Others point to individuals with a personal style as the true leaders of fashion, while others still continue to point out the historical significance of fashion leadership among the élite social and economic classes.

This 'trickle-down' theory of fashion leadership and adoption is an approach that has been widely accepted by many economists and sociologists including Thorstein Veblen, Gabriel Tarde and Georg Simmel; it is an approach that has received continuous support from both books on fashion history and from museum collections which continue to chronicle trends in fashion as changes in exclusive or élite fashions. Undoubtedly the 'noble' classes played an important role in fashion history, but in the changing social and economic environment of the twentieth century, it has become increasingly evident that fashion is not simply a matter of imitating a particular social or economic class.

FASHION AND SOCIAL STATUS

Historically, the people who had any choice in what they could wear – those who were not restricted by poverty, by their professions or even by sumptuary laws – were very small in number and often a close-knit group, so close, in fact, that they were often related to each other. For centuries, fashion respected this hierarchical system: members of each class wore clothes that were appropriate to that class and sumptuary laws forbade commoners to dress like nobles. Commoners were not allowed to wear the fabrics or carry the accessories of the upper classes, even if they could afford them. For centuries, fashion remained a luxurious and prestigious sign of rank and was largely confined to the nobility. Some articles of clothing betray their noble origins: the Norfolk jacket was named after the duke of that county; the Chesterfield coat (wool overcoat with a fitted waist and velvet collar) was named after Philip Stanhope, Earl

Diana, Princess of Wales. Her patronage of designers such as Bruce Oldfield did much to increase interest in British fashion designers.

women are largely unknown to us. And while they may be the élite and honoured guests at the designers' seasonal shows, the nature of *haute couture* and the domination of the

fashion industry by ready-to-wear means that the *couture* choices made by these twelve wealthy women do not necessarily influence fashion. The style of the Shiny Set may be commented on in the social pages of the glossy magazines but, by and large, most consumers look to other fashion leaders, and not necessarily individuals with exalted wealth. The trickle-down has dried up.

NEW FASHION LEADERS

The cultural industries – movies, television and popular music in particular – have led to new figures in fashion leadership emerging in the past fifty years. With the publicity surrounding them and their lifestyles, celebrities gain social prominence and their tastes or styles in dress become of equal interest. Like some members of the aristocracy, some stars have given their name to fashion items: the Hermes handbag, based on a saddle bag and launched in 1934, was renamed in 1955 the 'Kelly Bag' in honour of the American actress Grace Kelly, later Princess Grace of Monaco, who had popularized it. The Beatles, in the 1960s, gave their name to a hairstyle.

It is now equally important for designers to have 'stars' at their runway shows, either in the audience wearing last season's outfit or on the catwalk as a model, adding their seal of

French actress Catherine Deneuve, seen here with Yves Saint Laurent, is a former face of Chanel No 5 and remains a much sought-after guest at French designers' shows.

approval to the designer and the collection: Tina Turner at Azzedine Alaia, Barbra Streisand at Scasi, Elton John at Versace, Bianca Jagger at Calvin Klein, Eric Clapton at Giorgio Armani, Kylie Minogue at John Richmond, even John Hurt on the catwalk at Comme des Garçons. When Madonna visited the Cannes Film Festival, hundreds of French women, not her teenage fans, turned up to get a glimpse of her clothes. Her 1990 world tour featured the infamous pointed bras designed by Jean Paul Gaultier, while for the Girlie Show tour she turned to Italians Dolce e Gabbana and to Bob Mackie for her Marilyn Monroe-style outfit when she sang a song from the movie *Dick Tracy* at the 63rd Academy Awards ceremony. Following her first film *Desperately Seeking Susan* in 1984, thousands of Madonna's young fans copied her style and no doubt bought from a clothing company called Madonna Wannabe set up the same year. Even what Madonna wore when she went jogging was news and was copied, sadly by many who should have known better or at least should have taken up jogging.

The marketing potential of stars is such that many designers now loan entire ready-to-wear wardrobes in exchange for the stars' endorsement and some of the rubbed-off publicity that surrounds them.

FASHION AND POLITICS

For some celebrities, the decision to patronize a particular designer may not be out of personal choice but be politically motivated. Like Princess Diana's championing of British designers, the French Minister of Culture naturally chose French designers, Chanel in particular, when she went shopping. In 1909, Mrs Asquith, the wife of the British Prime Minister, invited Paul Poiret to show his collection at No. 10 Downing Street. Mrs Asquith and her husband were both censured for 'insulting' British trade and for even considering having foreign – particularly French – goods shown at a premises that essentially 'belonged' to the British taxpayer. Later, when Jacqueline Kennedy became America's First Lady, her public relations people ordered her out of the French houses of Givenchy, Chanel and Courrèges and told her to 'dress American'. Mrs. Kennedy's choice of American designer Oleg Cassini (he was in fact French by birth) proved fortunate. The designer obliged by providing a wardrobe that was almost identical to the clothes Mrs Kennedy would have bought in Paris: simple, top-stitched suits, pillbox hats (designed by Halston), black pump shoes and short white gloves (of which the First Lady had several hundred identical pairs), all of which were widely copied. When Bill Clinton was elected to the Oval Office, the US fashion industry held its breath as it waited for the news as to who would dress the new First Lady: Karan or Klein? When Hillary Clinton was photographed wearing a particular black dress with cut-away shoulders by Donna Karan, she

Politically correct: When Jacqueline Kennedy became America's First Lady, her public relations people ordered her to 'dress American': Oleg Cassini provided the answer.

was in good company: the very same dress was spotted in the same week by the press on Karan herself and on popular entertainer Liza Minelli.

MASS-PRODUCED FASHION

While there is no doubt that celebrities play a role in promoting designers and endorsing certain styles, it is not necessarily to these celebrities that designers look for ideas. In many instances, it is ordinary people who have given inspiration to the designers and it is possible to see how fashions have 'filtered-up', not only from youth to age, but from lower economic classes to the higher.

Typical fashions initiated by the young and less affluent are jeans – now every designer has their signature versions: t-shirts, biker jackets (which inspired Karl Lagerfeld for Chanel's top-selling ready-to-wear leather biker outfit from the autumn/winter 1992–93 collection), tracksuits (now a staple outfit from Calvin

Klein, Donna Karan and Ralph Lauren) and, finally, training shoes (available in designer versions by Che, Red or Dead or even with the interlocked 'C's of Chanel). A 1995 *Elle* fashion editorial remarked that the *ne plus ultra* in chic was to wear one's Sonia Rykiel evening dress with Birkenstock sandals – footwear that has been around for more than a hundred years and made popular not by fashion designers but by teenage skateboarders, vegetarians, 'natural shoe' enthusiasts and the rest of us who for years have refused to suffer painful feet.

What allows all sections of society to take part in the making of fashion and to wear what is currently 'in fashion' is the mass production of clothing and other items. Any new style – whether it comes from the top Paris, Milan, London, Tokyo or New York designers or from what young people are wearing on the streets of those cities – must be almost immediately mass-produced and widely retailed at a variety of price ranges, thereby ensuring its availability to all social and economic groups. Nevertheless, it is still much easier to describe what is 'in fashion' than to explain how it became fashion. But we do know that fashion doesn't just happen: it is triggered by people, by events, by social, economic and technological change. Most importantly, fashion isn't just what fashion designers put on the catwalks and what a handful of privileged élite or celebrities wear. Fashion is what we wear, a constant process of selection, adoption and change made by many – the fashion magazines in their highlighting of certain looks or styles, the retail buyers who stock the stores, the sales assistants who wear it, and us, the consumers who pick and choose from fashion. In a sort of post-modern bricolage, we assemble sometimes quite disparate units to re-create established looks or to 'create our own' individual ones.

Society at large is as much a part of the fashion industry as the famous designers who we sometimes credit too much with being the innovators of fashion.

'Filtered -up' fashion on the catwalk
at Jean Paul Gaultier

DRESSING FILMS AND TELEVISION

It is impossible to estimate just how far a film or a television star or any other 'media personality', by appearing in a particular designer's dress or suit, or perhaps simply through the use of an accessories such as sunglasses, a hairstyle or make-up detail, can provoke millions of imitations and create a 'fashion'. However, there is no question that the fashion world would be less influential without the television and cinema media. Few have the opportunity to see a live designer runway show in Paris or Milan, but millions will see the latest fashions on television and thousands will wear what they see. The clothes worn by TV and film stars legitimize and popularize current fashion trends; the media serve as a stage on which fashion designers' work gains visibility and social acceptance. The irony is that, while élite designer fashions have tried to keep their distance from high-street fashions, their very success depends on the popularization of styles in non-élite groups.

HOLLYWOOD AND THE FASHION INDUSTRY

In an interview in *Collier's Magazine* in 1931, the Hollywood producer Sam Goldwyn summed up the relationship of the movies with fashion and its designers when he predicted that women would go to the movies first, to see the film and the stars and second, to see the latest in clothes. Goldwyn himself had worked in the fashion industry – he had been a glove manufacturer – before turning to films. Marcus Loew and Adolphe Zukor had been in the fur trade and, while Zukor was at Paramount, he ordered that furs be used wherever possible, knowing that the widespread appeal of the stars would encourage sales in an industry that still employed most of his family.

In the earliest days of the Hollywood film industry, actors and actresses bought their own clothes or hired them. Some even hired out their wardrobes: D.W. Griffith, the director of *Birth of a Nation* (1915) and

Jean Harlow during filming of *Dinner at Eight*. The looks and fashions of the Hollywood stars were widely copied.

Gloria Swanson in a scene from *Tonight or Never* (1931) one of three movies for which the French couturier Coco Chanel designed costumes.

Intolerance (1916) is reputed to have told an actress that there was no part for her in one of his films but there was a part for her hat. It was duly hired at $5 (c. £3).

The great French *couture* houses were allowed roles also. Often, as publicity stunts or in an attempt to give their stars a more international appeal, the Hollywood studios sent their stars to Paris on shopping trips. In the 1930s, Pola Negri, Mary Pickford and Louise Brooks asked the big-name *couturiers* to design for them and the often enormous bills incurred were of little concern as it was all charged to the publicity accounts. On a visit to Paris in 1925, Gloria Swanson spent $250,000 (c. £156,000) on clothes and furs, mostly from leading *couturier* Jean Patou.

But many actresses did not get to keep these clothes: most ended up in the studio wardrobes to be modified and used again in different films. Women in audiences the world over thrilled with delight at the sight of Marlene Dietrich when she wore a $3500 (c. £2100) dress for just a few minutes in the 1937 film *Angel*. A solid mass of gold embroidery, emeralds, pearls and rubies edged with sable, the dress was too heavy to be placed on a coat hanger and had to be laid flat. It caused a storm on the set when the producers refused to give the dress to Dietrich for her personal wardrobe.

During the Depression of the early 1930s many formerly wealthy women, who had lost everything except their clothes, became movie extras and were rated according to their wardrobes. Once a year, every Hollywood extra took part in a dress parade held at the major studios. The women paraded before a critical panel of judges who classified the extras according to the clothes they wore. The 'dress extra' was the highest category and these women often had wardrobes that were the envy of many stars. The standard salary for a dress extra in the 1930s was $15 (c. £9) per day. Extras who had lines to say received $25 (c. £15).

As the Hollywood film industry grew, the clothes that were worn by the stars on screen began to be specially designed. Surprisingly, when Parisian *couturiers* were hired to do the job, they often failed to make the transition from *couturier* to costumier. Nevertheless, designers making the pilgrimage across the Atlantic to Hollywood included Elsa Schiaparelli, who designed for Mae West, Marcel Rochas, Jean Patou and Alix Grès. When introduced to Coco Chanel in 1929, Sam Goldwyn saw that Paris fashions offered an opportunity to lure his female audiences into movie houses. Goldwyn also realized that he had to be at the forefront of the latest trends in fashion after thousands of reels of film had to be thrown out: in 1929, Jean Patou

had suddenly dropped his hemlines and was instantly followed by all the other major designers. The fashions in Goldwyn's films that had been started in 1928 were now very much out of date.

While some studios sent scores of scouts and stylists to Paris to keep the studio bosses informed of the latest fashions, Goldwyn decided to bring a world-famous Paris *couturier* to Hollywood. Chanel's much-publicized stay in Hollywood was, in fact, much briefer than either she or Goldwyn had anticipated and she designed for just three

Delphine Seyrig, dressed by Coco Chanel, in *Last Year at Marienbad* (1961).

Rita Hayworth in the famous strapless dress designed by Jean Louis for *Gilda* (1946).

movies: *Palmy Days* (1931), a musical starring Eddie Cantor and Charlotte Greenwood, *Tonight or Never* (1931), starring Gloria Swanson, and *The Greeks Had a Word for It* (1932), starring Ina Claire. Despite the high profile of the movies, the stars and the designer, Chanel's clothes were either overlooked or criticized by the press for not being 'sufficiently Hollywood'. Although her initial foray into dressing films was disappointing, Chanel continued to design for films produced by French directors: Jean Renoir's *La Marseillaise* (1938) and *La Règle du Jeu* (1939), and Jean Cocteau's *La Machine Infernal* (1934). In 1961, Chanel returned to film to dress Romy Schneider for the 'Work' episodes in Luchino Visconti's *Boccaccio 70* and also designed for the gorgeous Delphine Seyrig in the Alain Renais film *Last Year at Marienbad* (1961).

From the late 1930s, the Hollywood studios began to shake off their dependence on Paris *couture* fashions and began to promote their own studio designers who 're-created' the fashions of the day and created some of their own fashion fads. Some of the Hollywood designers had *couture* training: Howard Greer started his fashion career with the English designer Lucile (Lady Duff-Gordon) and worked with Poiret and Molyneux before working at Paramount and RKO. Greer was also the first big-name costume designer to open a *couture* business

in Hollywood in 1927 and one of the first West Coast designers to establish his own wholesale business. Travis Banton had worked for the New York *couture* house of Madame Frances while Jean Louis was a Frenchman who arrived in New York in 1935 and worked for Hattie Carnegie as a designer. Louis' most famous Hollywood creation was the black strapless dress worn by Rita Hayworth for the 'Put The Blame on Mame' number in *Gilda* (1946). Although Hayworth maintained that the dress stayed up 'for two good reasons' it really stayed put because of Louis' skill as a *couturier*: he had incorporated pre-formed plastic bars in the bodice.

According to Hollywood's best-known film costume designer, Edith Head, Hollywood was never a fashion centre because it did not manufacture clothes to be purchased. Nevertheless, women's film magazines, such as *Women's Filmfare* (first published in 1934) and *Film Fashionland*, gave women advice on how to emulate the stars' beauty routines and dresses. The next step was to make the fashions seen on the screen available to ordinary women and many magazines offered paper patterns or ready-made screen-style dresses by post. One of the earliest specially designed film costumes to make an impact on the public was an outfit designed by Louis Garnier for actress Pearl White in the film *Plunder* (1923). The black suit and white blouse with a loose necktie, worn with a velour beret, was to become the uniform outfit of thousands of New York stenographers who were part of the new mass-market of working girls.

The most famous film outfit to have mass appeal is no doubt the Letty Lynton dress designed by Gilbert Adrian for Joan Crawford in the film of the same name. The dress was a major fashion hit and in 1932 Macy's of New York alone sold nearly half a million copies. Another Adrian success was the Eugenie hat he created for Greta Garbo in *Romance* (1930) which was copied by several manufacturers and sold to thousands of Garbo fans.

COSMETICS CONNECTIONS

Both television and cinema have been responsible for creating countless 'looks' and 'fads', as well as fashions. Hollywood's effects on the cosmetics industry is significant. Although skincare preparations and face powders were commonly used by most women, visible make-up such as lipsticks, eyeshadows, rouge and nail polish were largely confined to theatrical use and continued to be associated with the 'painted ladies' of ill repute. The turning point in the public's acceptance of colourful, visible, make-up came with Hollywood's manufacture of female screen stars.

In 1917, the actress Theda Bara went to one of the leading cosmetics experts, Helena Rubinstein, in order to find a way to emphasize her eyes, which looked too small on screen. Rubinstein offered mascara, then unknown in the US and only used in France by a few stage actresses, and some colour for her

eyelids. The sensational effects were reported in every newspaper and magazine in America. Other actresses went to Max Factor, a former wig-maker from Russia who, as the line in the song 'Hooray for Hollywood' states, was reputedly able to 'make a monkey look good'. Initially, cosmetics were produced specifically for the film industry: grease-paint (the forerunner of modern foundation creams), lip-gloss (previously actresses had to lick their lips between shots), eyeshadows, mascaras and false eyelashes. But the demand by the public for the 'looks' Factor created for actresses was

When Theda Bara complained that her eyes looked too small on screen, Helena Rubenstein introduced her to mascara and eyehadow, products then largely unknown in the US.

so great that he began to sell his cosmetics commercially. Max Factor's development of water-soluble pancake make-up in 1938 was a major turning point in the acceptance of colourful make-up, such as Italian *couturier* Elsa Schiaparelli's outrageous shade Shocking Pink. Max Factor's products were also promoted using film stars to project the idea of glamour, a device still in use today.

The cosmetic industry boomed and, since the 1960s, it has been one of the few growth industries in western economies. With the drop in income from *haute couture* in the 1960s, many of the European fashion houses ventured into cosmetics: Dior, Chanel and Yves Saint Laurent all have beauty products and cosmetics as part of their extended lines.

The media and male cosmetics

As the female market became saturated with products, cosmetic companies turned their attention to men. Despite conservative resistance to the very idea, sales of face cleansers, moisturizers, lip-glosses (though they are marketed as 'lip-balms' of the type used by outdoor pursuit sportsmen) and even blemish concealers and foundation creams have risen steadily. However, while much effort has gone into developing skincare products, deodorants and haircare products for the men's market, the most lucrative market area is still, particularly for the fashion designer, in the area of aftershaves and men's colognes.

One aspect of the electronic media's influence on fashion that is often overlooked is

Capturing the male market: designers have used figures from outside fashion, such as Manchester United and France footballer Eric Cantona, in order to appeal to the male fashion consumer.

in the area of televised sports. This has undoubtedly helped many players to gain celebrity outside of their sport and the names of famous sportsmen and women endorse fashions and accessories for on and off the field, for example, Fred Perry, Lacoste and even Nick Faldo, whose signature aftershave Golf Club is packaged in a golf club-shaped bottle. In Britain, the major soccer clubs almost annually launch new team uniforms secure in the knowledge that thousands of their fans will purchase and wear them at matches and as casual wear. Thousands will also see international soccer celebrities like Eric Cantona modelling the latest in designer ready-to-wear in magazines like *GQ* and *Arena* and even making appearances on the catwalks of international designer shows.

Because of the visibility through television of sporting events like the Olympics, sports clothes, both in their design and in their fibre and construction technology, have influenced the design of clothing worn by amateur and professional athletes as well as 'non-sport' clothes which draw their inspiration from sportswear, like fashion training shoes and fashion swimwear.

THE MEDIA AND THE CONSUMER

One phenomenon that grew out of Hollywood was its creation of stars that usurped the role played by the traditional élite and aristocratic customers of fashion. From the earliest years of this century, film and, later, television, gave us new fashion role models. In Hollywood's golden years, fashion consumers looked to Garbo's tweeds, Jean Harlow's platinum-blonde hair, Joan Crawford's lips and Dietrich's plucked eyebrows. And when Clark Gable took of his shirt in *It Happened One Night* in 1934 to reveal a bare chest, sales of men's undershirts plummeted.

What we see on the screen or on television becomes almost instantly desired and the history of fashion is littered with numerous examples of films' influence on what we wear:

Elizabeth Taylor's satin and lace slip in *Butterfield 8* (1960) created a sensation and volume sales. Marlon Brandon and James Dean did much to popularize Levi fly button 501 jeans and white t-shirts, so much so that this humble shirt has been the biggest selling item of clothing since World War II. In 1967, *Bonnie and Clyde* brought pinstripes back into style while in 1974 *The Great Gatsby* catapulted its costume designer Ralph Lauren into the limelight: 'I've never seen such beautiful shirts' says Mia Farrow to Robert Redford as he tosses several dozen into the air. Three years later, Lauren dressed Diane Keaton in *Annie Hall* and the baggy pants, floppy hat

By the 1950s the T-shirt had became a staple of the American youth wardrobe, popularized by movie stars like Marlon Brando in *The Wild One*.

The look of Armani's costumes for *The Untouchables* also appeared in the designer's ready-to-wear range: five button waistcoats, seam-to-seam trousers and three-piece suits.

and oversized waistcoat look was born.

In the 1980s, while *Fame* and *Flashdance* cashed in on the dance craze and encouraged the wearing of ripped sweatshirts and legwarmers as daywear, Giorgio Armani reinvented the 1930s in *The Untouchables* and introduced five-button waistcoats, creaseless seam-to-seam trousers and three-piece suits. But the ultimate symbol of yuppie consumer culture as reflected by the mass media has to be the Gordon Gekko shirt, the horizontally-striped shirt with white collar and cuffs, named after Michael Douglas's character Gordon 'Lunch is for wimps' Gekko in *Wall Street*. Douglas's suits for this movie were from Nino Cerruti, who also designed for Jack Nicholson in *The Witches of Eastwick*.

Promo-costuming

Even more obvious than the high fashion of these films is the influence of film and television characters in the area of children's clothing; *Superman*, *Batman*, *The Incredible Hulk* and *Power Rangers* have all proven to be highly profitable marketing devices.

One of the most recent developments in the fashion–film relationship has been 'promo-costuming', where a well-known fashion designer has produced an entire ready-to-wear costume collection for a film and for sale. A successful film is good advertising for the designer and recent examples of promo-costuming have included Jean Paul Gaultier's for *The Cook, The Thief, His Wife and Her Lover* (1989) and Oscar de la Renta's for the brat-pack movie *Bright Lights, Big City* (1988). The pattern seems also to have spilled over into television: sit-com *Murphy Brown* star Candice Bergen's character wears the ready-to-wear lines of Donna Karan.

Television personalities, whether actors or talk-show presenters, are all feted to play a part in promoting contemporary fashions. Most often, it is the female stars who play the leading role: Oprah Winfrey on one occasion devoted an entire show to celebrating Donna Karan's first ten years with a live catwalk presentation, commentary by Karan, plus interviews with stars who also wore her clothes. Another *Oprah* show was devoted to fashions selected by supermodel Cindy Crawford. Meanwhile millions of viewers are able to watch Oprah herself talk and demonstrate her own fashion successes (and mistakes). Contemporary daytime television constantly provides viewers – young and old, male and female – with fashion tips and the once-in-a-lifetime opportunity to be 'made over' by the professionals.

Once in a while the clothes worn by a television personality spark off a fashion, as in the case of the Nehru jacket which Johnny Carson wore on *The Tonight Show* in 1968. Within the next few weeks, thousands of men across the US bought the same jacket. Nolan Miller successfully launched his Dynasty Collection, a ready-to-wear line based on his designs that could be seen weekly by viewers of *Dynasty*. The show also launched scents like Forever Krystal and the men's cologne Carrington, both named after characters in the television soap opera. Not to be outdone, actress Joan Collins who also starred in the show threw her name behind designer jeans and her own perfume, Spectacular.

Such is the power of the mass media and of celebrity that the heroes and heroines of fictional television shows about the rich and glamorous have their impact on fashion.

Television gave us the detective series *Miami Vice*, and its two male leads influenced men's casual dress for years, popularizing designer stubble and t-shirts under unconstructed jackets. *American Bandstand* (which debuted in 1957 in America), followed by British programmes like *Ready Steady Go* and *Top of the Pops* have through the years constantly provided youth audiences with an opportunity to see their idols and their clothes on television. In recent years, the music video has spawned numerous fashion influences as youngsters try to look like their idols, adopting styles worn by Madonna or the urban rap and hip-hop artists. The great importance of music videos and television was acknowledged in 1988 when MTV received an award from the Council of Fashion Designers of America for its influence on fashion. MTV continues to shape a new generation of fashion through its *House of Style* programme hosted by supermodel Cindy Crawford.

Television, like the movies and other mass media, not only popularizes current fashion trends but serves as a vehicle by which new designs become visible. But status symbols such as designer clothes, when so widely diffused and accepted will eventually fade in popularity. As they lose their false cachet of exclusivity, the fashions will be replaced by brand new 'objects of desire'.

The cast of *Dynasty*, one of the most popular television shows of the 1980s. Costume designer Nolan Miller would launch the 'Dynasty Collection', a ready-to-wear line based on the outfits worn by the characters in the show.

MANUFACTURERS AND SUPPLIERS

Fashion producers divide into two broad categories: the primary markets which provide us with fabrics – the raw material of fashion, and the secondary markets which manufacture finished garments. It must be remembered however, that these two categories depend on each other, on the designer or design teams and ultimately, on the consumer.

THE GLOBAL TEXTILE INDUSTRY

Every textile product starts its life as a fibre – either a natural fibre, such as cotton, linen, silk and wool, which can come from plant or animal sources, or a synthetic fibre which is produced by a chemical process. Either way, once a fibre has been bought by a textile manufacturer, it undergoes the same basic processes of spinning into yarn, weaving or knitting into fabric and finally, the finishing processes to give it colour, texture, pattern and perhaps a special finish such as fire or water-proofing.

Textiles are among the world's oldest products; in 1980, it was estimated that the US alone provided enough linear yards of fabric to wrap around the earth more than 250 times. Yet the US industry has lost 50 per cent of its domestic market due to fierce competition from imports over the last fifteen years. In addition to large growth in the textile industries of Japan, other Pacific Rim countries and India, the removal of trade barriers in 1992 when Europe became an integrated economic community produced a European textile industry larger than that of the US. Furthermore, it is acknowledged that European centres, where traditional craftsmanship is highly valued, lead in textile innovation in both production techniques and in styling.

Today the textile industry includes companies that carry out all the processes of production and distribution, from spinning to selling the fabrics to manufacturers. Some Italian textile companies like Gruppo Gft in Turin are manufacturers as well, making parts of Giorgio Armani and Valentino ready-to-wear lines. There are, however, many companies, both large and small, that continue to specialize in only one phase of production, for example, spinning, weaving, knitting, printing or converting. A converter is

The Hugo Boss factory. The German fashion company became internationally known in the 1980s when their men's ready-to-wear was featured in US soaps *Dallas* and *Dynasty*.

a textile company that buys or handles griege (pronounced 'gray') goods or unfinished, usually woven, cloth which then goes to different types of finishing plants for bleaching, dyeing or printing. Most often, converters own neither fabric mills nor finishing factories, but serve as middlemen between the two stages of production. As such, converters keep in touch with the clothing manufacturers to find out fashion trends – the colours, textures, patterns and finishes that are likely to be next year's fashion statements.

In some instances in the US, textile producers, apparel manufacturers and garment retailers have formed co-operative alliances via EDI, the Electronic Data Interchange. All

The designer's name suggests that we are buying something unique, even though it is, in fact, mass produced.

goods are given a UPC (universal product code), a bar code which identifies style, colour, size, price, fabrication, and vendor. When the garment is retailed, its coded information is sent via EDI to the retail buyer who will order new stock, to the garment manufacturer who will cut more garments in that size, colour, fabric and style, and to the textile manufacturer who will send more of that colour fabric to the garment manufacturer. While this system works well for volume manufacture of basic garments, at the designer level of the market where smaller quantities are manufactured, the enormous financial outlay required for the technology may not be so readily available or so quickly recouped.

MATERIALS FOR FASHION DESIGN
Natural and synthetic fibres

Before the appearance of synthetic fibres, the suppliers of natural fibres – cotton, wool, linen and silk – were not really part of the fashion industry. Traditionally, the suppliers raised a crop or flock, sold the raw materials at the local market and then disappeared until the next crop or flock was harvested. Now, through associations such as the International Institute for Cotton, the International Wool Secretariat, the Silk Institute and the International Linen Promotion, natural fibre producers act as a source of information for designers and manufacturers about their respective fibres and about developments in weaves, patterns and colours. These associations also publicize their fibres to the

trade, the press and the retail stores and undertake co-operative advertising with makers and sellers of garments in their fibres. The International Wool Secretariat, for example, encourages producers and retailers to use the Woolmark logo in the advertising of fashion garments made of wool.

For centuries, people struggled to duplicate, either mechanically or chemically, what nature appears to produce effortlessly, but it was not until 1884 that the French Count Hilaire de Chardonet developed a fibre that was called 'artificial silk'. In 1925 this fibre was re-named Rayon. Throughout the 1920s and 1930s, rayon was followed by a whole host of new synthetic fibres. The biggest breakthrough came in 1939 at the Golden Gate Exposition in San Francisco when the giant chemical company DuPont gave its first public showing of hosiery made of nylon. A whole new world of textiles – of acrylics, polyesters, triacetates, modacrylics and spandex – have been successfully launched and marketed under brand names like 'Golden Glow' (polyester made by American Enka), 'Colouray' (rayon by Courtaulds) and 'Trevira' (polyester by Hoechst). Where would the Olympics be today with the support of 'Lycra' (spandex by DuPont)?

Unlike suppliers of natural fibre, the synthetic fibre producers made fashion their business right from the start. It was the textile industry that knew how to handle these fibres and educated spinners, weavers and knitters in their processing and handling. But they also had to create a demand among consumers. In short, they not only provided the fibres but, with the resources of a huge industry, they were able to assume the dominant role in determining how these fibres were to be used in yarns, fabrics and fashion clothing.

If paint is the artist's medium, fabric is the fashion designer's palette, and most large producers keep large fabric libraries located in the major fashion centres. These libraries, which designers visit, keep samples of fabric from every mill or converter using their fibres. If a designer is looking for a particular fabric, the library can help locate the mill or converter that makes it. Twice a year the most important showcases for fabrics are held in Europe to exhibit fabrics to designers and manufacturers. In March and October in Paris there is *Premier Vision*, literally the first look at new fashion fabrics. In April and October or November in Frankfurt in Germany there is Interstoff (short for International Fabrics) and at Como in Italy there is *Ideacomo* (Ideas from Como) which primarily exhibits Italian silks. In December and June in Paris is *Nouvelles Rencontres* (New Meetings) which is primarily organized to appeal to manufacturers looking for fashion ideas. There are also fabric shows in London, and in New York and Los Angeles, where fashion lines are officially presented four times a year.

LEATHER

Textiles and fibre producers are not the only providers of raw materials to the fashion

From hide to finished design: leather goods at the House of Hermes where each handbag is produced by hand.

industry: leather suppliers also play their part. Leather has always been important for accessories such as shoes, belts and handbags, but, particularly since the rise of Italian ready-to-wear designers in the late 1960s and 1970s, leather has become increasingly important for outerwear fashions. An essential ingredient in leather processing is time: in spite of mechanization, it still takes several weeks to transform a hide into flexible leather which is the colour, texture and weight required for the various aspects of the fashion garment industry. Because of the length of time involved, it is two years before the customer sees the finished leather end-product on sale in retail stores.

At the annual leather show *Semaine de Cuir* (Leather Week) held in Paris each

September, tanners from all over the world present their offerings in steer, cow and bull hides, calfskin and kidskin (the skin of large calves or small breeds of cattle), sheepskins and lambskins, goat and kidskins, equine skins (horse, colt, ass, mule and zebra hides), buffalo, pig, hog and boar leathers, ostrich skins and reptile skins (alligator, crocodile, lizard and snakeskin). While this might sound like wholesale animal slaughter simply for our vanity, bear in mind that much leather is the by-product of the meat farming industry. It is also worth noting that the population of the United States alone wears out more than 400 million pairs of shoes, sandals, boots and slippers a year. Footwear is the area of largest volume production with more than 7 billion pairs of shoes produced world-wide each year. Yet despite constant demand, some respected manufacturers like Clark's Shoes in Britain have felt the cold wind of recession coupled with cheap foreign imports bite into their companies.

To help coordinate clothing with footwear, fashion designers attend leather shows: Lineapelle in Bologna in May and November, and MIDEC (Mode International de la Chausseur) in Paris in March and October. Traditionally, it is the expensive shoes that have come from Europe: Maud Frizon, Stephane Keilan and Charles Jourdan from France, Bruno Magli and Salvatore Ferragamo from Italy, which is also where the fashion shoe company Joan and David are still using the Martini factories, among the oldest and

finest in Italy. Fashion designers such as Valentino, Jean Paul Gaultier, Donna Karan and Yves Saint Laurent also license their designs to shoe manufacturers.

The price of a shoe depends primarily on the quality of leather, the workmanship and the amount of detailing, but many companies are able to make a bigger mark-up because of the popularity of their name or a designer license. Once, we were not brand-loyal to shoes, but since the fashion has emerged for training shoes and 'grunge' styles which popularized large comfortable boots, Nike, Reebok, Dr Marten's and Caterpillars are footwear that we now ask for by name and consistently repurchase.

Cheaper shoes, including designer 'knock-offs' or copies, are available from Brazil (particularly leather shoes), Korea (for sports shoes) and Taiwan (for fabric shoes). Quite possibly the most copied shoe of recent times has been Patrick Cox's Wannabe loafer.

CENTRES OF FASHION PRODUCTION

For the majority of shoppers, the fashions we buy are essentially mass-produced. Fashion is one of France's top three export industries and employs more people than its automobile industry. Surprisingly, much of the upper end of French *prêt-à-porter* is manufactured in Italy, though mainstream ready-to-wear is still produced in the Sentier district, the old clothing manufacturing area of Paris. In Italy, the fashion industry is devoted primarily to '*moda pronta*' with Milan at its centre because of the city's proximity to the fabric sources at Turin, Como and Biella. Italian designers, manufacturers and fashion companies often work together to minimize risks and many Italian fashion companies are still largely family-owned, for instance, knitwear designers Ronita and Tai Missoni, the Fendi sisters, and Salvatore Ferragamo's children who have expanded their father's business into accessories and ready-to-wear. In addition, the large textile firms are able to invest heavily in new technology, and it is for these three reasons that Italy is able to maintain its reputation as a world-class fashion producer and fashion centre.

London has earned its present ranking as a fashion capital largely as a result of the rise of British youth culture and fashion in the 1960s. Since that heady time of the 'Swinging Sixties', British fashion designers have faced a constant uphill struggle for the recognition, financial backing and organized promotion that their contemporaries in Europe enjoy. Despite the fact that the British clothing industry employs over half a million people nationwide, many British ready-to-wear designers have their garments produced in Italy or the Far East. It should be noted also that many of Britain's best-known contemporary designers are not in fact British: Nicole Farhi is French, Joseph Ettedgui is Morrocan, Rifat Ozbek is Turkish and John Rocha is Chinese with an Irish accent. Nevertheless, Britain continues to attract

Italian designers, manufacturers and fashion companies often work together to minimise risk. Many companies, like Benetton, are largely family owned.

foreign buyers for home-grown talents like Vivienne Westwood, Katharine Hamnett, Jasper Conran, Betty Jackson, Bruce Oldfield and the late Jean Muir, as well as shoppers seeking that quintessentially 'English' look

Haute couture for men: Savile Row in London is synonymous with bespoke tailoring. A Savile Row suit may involve up to 150 separate hand operations and take up to four weeks to complete.

made of Burberry and Aquascutum trenchcoats and woolly jumpers or that certain look known as 'street style', comprising a post-modern assemblage of tartan, punk and Birkenstock sandals.

London is still a respected fashion capital particularly when it comes to one particular type of clothing: the bespoke or custom-tailored man's suit from Savile Row, even though today many Savile Row tailors are not even located on this street. A Savile Row suit may involve as many as 150 separate and distinct hand operations and take between three and four weeks to complete; it can set

the well-dressed gentleman customer back as much as £5000 (c. $8000). As well as a choice between three variations of the basic silhouette and single or double-breasted jackets, the bespoke-suit customer can choose among a number of famous names including Gieves and Hawkes, tailors to many male members of European royal families, Henry Poole (the oldest Savile Row firm) and 'new kid on the block' Richard James. Already highly respected, James's work brings together the traditions of quality tailoring with an *avant-garde* aesthetic that epitomizes the very best of British fashion and style.

In menswear, it was traditionally brand names that were better known and assumed to be of more importance to the male consumer. Today designers that became successful largely through women's wear are becoming increasingly important in menswear. The new world of menswear is now designer-name led, largely the result of licensing agreements between designers and manufacturers: Hart Schaffner and Marx are the licensed manufacturers for Christian Dior, Nino Cerruti and Pierre Cardin amongst others, while the giant Bidermann Industries are the licensed manufacturers for Yves Saint Laurent and Calvin Klein Tailored Clothing.

In the US, New York City remains at the heart of American fashion. Historically the home of garment manufacturing, today nearly two-thirds of American manufacturing – fashion showrooms, design studios, and manufacturers' headquarters and showrooms – are still located in the city and most of it takes place on Seventh Avenue between 34th and 40th Street. At 550 Seventh Avenue are the high-fashion companies, including Bill Blass, Donna Karan and Oscar de la Renta. At 1400 Broadway the 'Junior Miss' (teen to young adult fashions) manufacturers can be found; the home of women's daywear is at 1407, 1410 and 1411 Broadway, while at 1290 Avenue of the Americas – better known to most people as the Empire State Building – you'll find offices for the manufacturing base of 75 per cent of all men's clothing in America. At one time the actual manufacturers of American fashion also had their production facilities in the city as well, but rising costs both of land and labour have led many to source producers and labour forces in Asia and other parts of the world.

After each manufacturer's collection or line is designed, it must be presented to the retail buyers. In Europe the ready-to-wear shows are held twice a year: in March (for autumn/winter of the following year) and October (for spring/summer of the following year) in Paris (*Pret-a-Porter Feminin*), Milan (*Milanovendamoda*), and in London (London Fashion Week). February and September see men's ready-to-wear in Paris and Milan, while childrenswear collections are shown February and September in Paris and January and June in Florence. Nevertheless the traditional marketplaces in Europe are now under stiff competition: January also sees Tokyo Fashion Week and Hong Kong Fashion Week, while March and October bring Munich Fashion Week and IGEDO in Düsseldorf, the world's largest fashion market with manufacturers from over a hundred countries showing their collections. Add to this the fact that the American designers show their collections five times a year and it is no surprise that at any time, somewhere in the world, there is a fashion show taking place. Each collection presented has the potential to be either the look of the season or the collection that brings financial disaster for manufacturers and ruin for designers.

EXTENDED RANGE

The *haute couture* houses still present their sumptuous creations twice-yearly in Paris before the international press and they still enjoy their illustrious reputation, yet *haute couture* in the period after World War II gradually ceased to be the focal point of fashion. By 1975, made-to-order operations counted for less than 20 per cent of direct profits of the *couture* houses. Ten years later, profits were further squeezed to 10 per cent. The number of people employed in *couture* is also indicative of the changed fortunes of this section of the industry. In the 1920s, Jean Patou employed more than a thousand people in his *couture* workshops; before World War II Coco Chanel employed 2,500 workers, while Christian Dior in the mid-1950s had over a thousand employees all engaged solely in the production of made-to-order fashions. By 1985, the remaining 21 houses classified as '*couture-creation*' employed only 2,000 workers between them, providing *haute couture* clothing for fewer than 3,000 customers world-wide.

By the 1980s, *couture* designers had fully realized that they had to find new ways of

increasing their revenue and had come to terms with the fact that a large part of their income came, in fact, from the sale of their designs to the mass market rather than their private customers. Today, the *haute couture* houses remain profitable largely through their ready-to-wear lines, licensing deals and loss leaders like perfumes and cosmetics.

What the Americans were first to call ready-to-wear, the French call *prêt-à-porter* in an attempt to signify this product's difference from 'manufactured' clothing which had a poor reputation. Manufactured clothing was often marked by defects in cuts, poor-quality finishing and an overall lack of imagination. Ready-to-wear attempted to marry industry with fashion.

EARLY *PRÊT-À-PORTER*

Some aspects of ready-to-wear fashion made their appearance first in the 1920s: the economic crisis brought about by the Wall

Street Crash in 1929 had a profound effect on the European fashion industry. With no American buyers in Paris in 1931 and the absence from the mid-1930s of private American customers (upon whom the Paris *couturiers* increasingly depended), the designers were forced into new profit making ventures. *Toiles* – the canvas, linen or calico copies of *couture*-model garments – began to be made and sold for copying purposes. 'Wholesale *couture*' could now be offered by wholesale manufacturers like Jaeger, Dereta and Dorville. The problem with this system was that it was an open door to the pirates. Chief among the villains were the Germans and Americans who hired teams of people to memorize particular aspects of a collection or even parts of garments they saw at the Paris houses and then, back in the privacy of their hotel rooms, the teams would recreate the garments and produce accurate sketches to be sent to the manufacturers. These copies became the department-store models which in turn, were themselves copied even more crudely by the cheaper end of the market.

Today, while private customers and the press are admitted free of charge to *couture* shows, most houses insist that trade buyers pay a 'caution' (a deposit of surety). This is a 'right-to-see' payment that in some houses takes the form of a minimum required purchase, usually one or two models. The caution is then deducted from the total amount of purchases made. If there is no purchase or if the total spent does not equal the caution (which can be as high as $6,000) there is no refund. Furthermore, trade buyers are usually charged a higher price for a garment than private customers since the *couture* house maintains that the retailer and producers are actually buying copying rights as well as the original garment.

Before the 1960s, ready-to-wear garments were essentially watered-down versions of *haute couture* collections; the 1960s was the last decade in which *haute couture* would have an impact on ready-to-wear, through its sanctioning of trousers and the mini-skirt in *couture* showings by Andre Courrèges, Cristobal Balenciaga and Yves Saint Laurent.

THE RISE AND RISE OF READY-TO-WEAR

Ready-to-wear came into its own in the 1960s when clothes were created that reflected the novel, youthful and daring spirit of the age rather than attempting to reproduce cheaper versions of *haute couture* fashions that were themselves associated with an increasingly small élite, so small in fact that *haute couture* today is simply a vehicle for advertising one's wealth rather than one's fashion sense. The rise of ready-to-wear was also aided by a growing band of new young designers who were, for the first time, not part of the world of *haute couture*: Danielle Hechter, Cacharel, Mary Quant, Emmanuelle Khan and Elie Jacobson (Dorothy Bis).

Fashion and mass production have combined in France to produce a ready-to-wear industry of around 3,000 garment-producing firms, about 205 of which are devoted to menswear. The womenswear industry alone is believed to employ some 90,000 people. Nevertheless, the serious challenge to Paris's supremacy came and continues to come from Italy which has been attracting foreign buyers since the 1950s.

In addition to quality workmanship, Italy has developed a reputation for innovative styling in knitwear, accessories (notably in leather) and for menswear. The Italian *moda pronta* industry, unlike its French counterpart, developed simultaneously with its *haute couture* industry and did not depend on Italian couturiers for fashion leadership and design talent. Originally, the semi-annual showings of *moda pronta* were presented in Florence, in the elegant surroundings of the Pitti Palace, but in the mid-1970s, ready-to-wear firms in the north of Italy began presenting in Milan. The initial handful of companies like Basile, Callaghan and Missoni grew steadily and today the other famous Italian ready-to-wear firms like Pucci, Gianni Versace, Giorgio Armani, Krizia and Complice all show in Milan.

The experience of Italian *couture* designers nevertheless parallels that of the Paris houses: a dwindling ultra-rich clientele and few trade buyers means that the largely unprofitable *couture* operations are subsidized by ready-to-wear, accessories, perfumes and other goods to which the designer's name adds prestige.

No longer a driving force in fashion, *haute*

With the upper end of ready-to-wear almost as expensive as some *couture* collections, designers have extended their lines to create 'bridge collections'.

couture finally understood how valuable ready-to-wear could be when it was coupled with its own history and tradition of prestige

73

and exclusivity. In 1959, Pierre Cardin presented the first ready-to-wear collection at the Printemps department store in Paris and claimed to have launched a 'Popular National Theatre' of fashion. In 1963, Cardin opened his first ready-to-wear department and was the first *couturier* to sign agreements with major ready-to-wear manufacturers, exploiting the prestige of the designer-name label. In 1966, Yves Saint Laurent created the first ready-to-wear collection conceived not as an adaptation of *haute couture*, but wholly in terms of industrial production. At the same time he opened his first Rive Gauche boutique and, in 1983–4, the Saint Laurent's Variation line was launched with prices up to 40 per cent less than Rive Gauche.

By 1985, women's ready-to-wear amounted to over 30 per cent of the *couture* houses' profits. But it was not only women's fashions that were undergoing change: once again under the leadership of Pierre Cardin, a new focus for French couturiers was provided with their own seasonal presentations of men's ready-to-wear lines. What at first to many appeared to be simply a passing fad, men's ready-to-wear has in fact turned out to be growth market: in 1975, it accounted for nearly 10 per cent of the *couture* houses' profits and by 1985 it was nearly 20 per cent.

WHAT'S IN A (DESIGNER'S) NAME?

In the 1970s, the designer label became attached to an item of clothing that had begun its life as practical workwear and in the 1960s had become synonymous with middle-class youth rebelling from the restrictions of conformity. Designer jeans were born and when Calvin Klein was the first to market signature jeans in 1978, more than 200,000 pairs were sold in the first few weeks, even though they cost up to 50 per cent more than a pair of Levis. By 1984 sales of Calvin Klein jeans had netted the designer an estimated $400 (c. £250) million. Other designers followed suit, though some were not quite as successful as they might have hoped. The key players in the designer jeans market today remain Calvin Klein, Giorgio Armani, Donna Karan, Guess?, The Gap and Gianni Versace, whose advertising of Versace Jeans Couture demonstrates just how powerful the idea of the 'exclusive' designer signature can be when it is applied to thousands of pairs of jeans.

Ready-to-wear has succeeded in making widespread the symbol of distinction that was once accessible to only the very few: the designer label. In the 1920s, Jean Patou put his initial on the outside of his clothes and in the 1950s Emilio Pucci began adding his signature to his printed fabric designs. The power of the designer's name – whether dead or alive – is such that it is now almost a license to print money; every item from underwear to eyewear, wrist watches to cigarettes is licensed out to generate income. One of the most recent examples is provided by British shoe designer Patrick Cox and Italian motorcycle manufacturer Italjet who have teamed up to

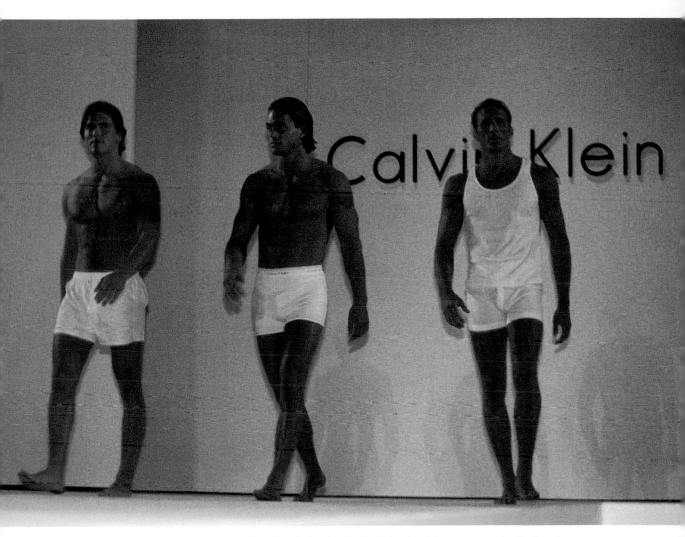

Once upon a time, underwear was considered largely functional attire. Today, the designer name makes it a less obscure object of desire.

produce the ultimate designer runaround: the Wannabee Velocifero scooter complete with 1960s-inspired op art finish, Wannabe logo on the front and rear panels and matching seat and helmet in Cox's signature black and white faux-python skin. Cost £2000 (c. $3200).

Where once the anonymity of a woman's wardrobe was jealously guarded and the only label was the one sewn discreetly into the armpit seam, we now wear designer name, initials and logos emblazoned across our chests, like medieval knights carrying their shields marked with their coat of arms, signalling our allegiance to one or other fashion monarch.

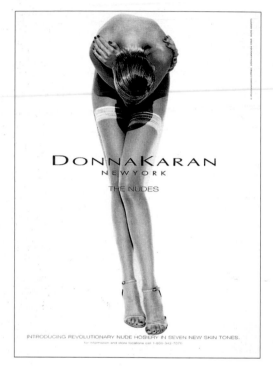

Hosiery by Donna Karan. It is now possible to be dressed from top to toe in designer name ready-to-wear – and to buy a range of designer cosmetics and perfumes to create the total look.

LICENSING AND DIFFUSION LINES

Our desire to be walking advertisements for various designers has been fuelled by two developments: the introduction of diffusion lines by ready-to-wear designers and the growing trend in licensing designer names. Today's ready-to-wear creations can now cost almost as much as a *couture* garment. A relatively simple *couture* garment may cost between $2000 (c. £1250) and $10,000 (c. £6250), and be for the most part exclusive and made to measure. The upper end of the ready-to-wear market now charges roughly between $1500 (c. £930) and $7000 (c. £4400) for an off-the-peg, mass-produced garment. Despite the designer label, designer ready-to-wear does not bring *couture* exclusivity, but the prices do not make it universally affordable. Very few can easily afford to wear a Giorgio Armani jacket priced at £1000 (c. $1600). But more of us can wear a Mani by Giorgio Armani jacket at £500 (c. $800) and even more can afford an Emporio Armani jacket at £150 (c. $240). Most ready-to-wear designers have introduced diffusion lines, or 'bridge collections' as they are sometimes known, as they recognize that the world is full of potential customers: Donna Karan and DKNY, Jean-Paul Gaultier and Junior Gaultier, Jean Muir and Jean Muir Studio, Karl Lagerfeld and KL, Anne Klein and Anne Klein II. And if we still can't afford to wear the clothes, we can cover ourselves in the designer fragrance.

Our consumer-driven society holds change and novelty as sacred and asserts that the search for instant happiness and identity in a mass society is crucial to our personal

Right: The advertisement for Donna Karan's diffusion line DKNY over New York's Times Square used the city's skyline as its theme and became part of that skyline itself.

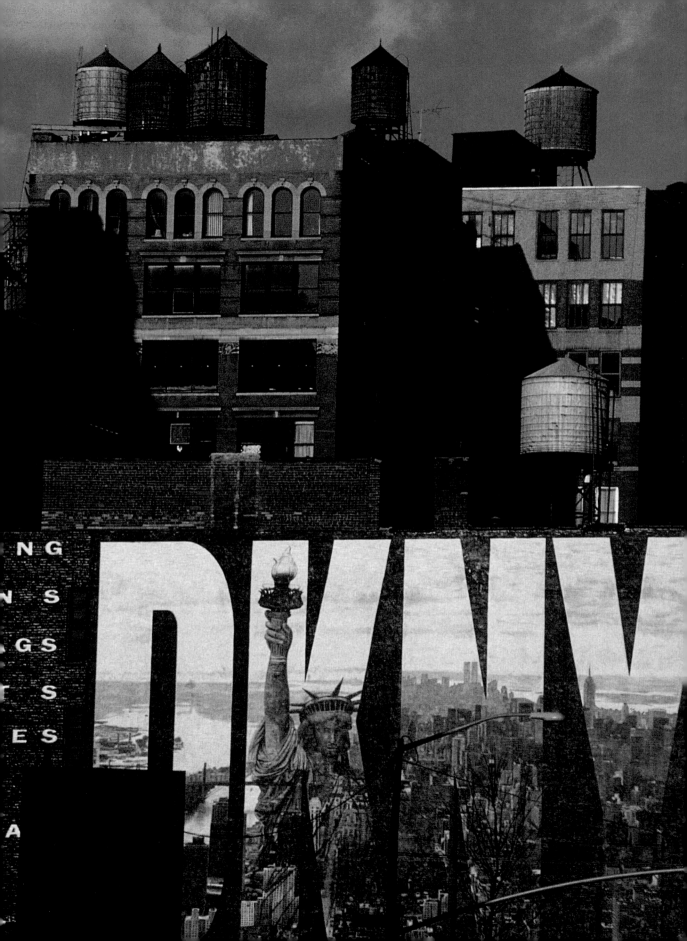

development. Fashion design has done its best to fulfil these demands. Wholesale licensing has made the transient signs of fashion accessible to all: today, licenses cover every conceivable product and provide a means of diversification for designers without the risk of capital investment or the responsibility of manufacture. Licenses make it possible for designers to produce a range of coats, swimwear, cosmetics and accessories that they could not produce in their own companies because of the lack of expertise or capital. The eyewear and sunglasses market is today reckoned to be worth an estimated $1 billion a year and very few designers have missed this market. Fees to designers, often solely for the use of their name, provides them and their companies with incomes that in some cases are larger than the gross national product of some Third World countries: Ralph Lauren's estimated turnover at the beginning of the 1990s was $1,500,000,000; Gianni Versace's $480,000,000; Calvin Klein's $200,000,000 and Donna Karan's $240,000,000. The king of the licenses remains Pierre Cardin with more than 800 licenses including bicycle pumps and baby buggies, while Oscar de la Renta has papayas on his list of licenced products. Licensing therefore does not mean that the designer has designed the product: it may simply imply approval of a design. For the astute businessperson, licensing can be a license to print money.

THE SWEET SMELL OF SUCCESS

Today, the designer's name is simply another brand name used to penetrate the mass market. The practice of licensing first became widespread in the 1940s and 1950s when Christian Dior licensed his name to hoisery, glove and shoe manufacturers, but it first began in the 1920s when Coco Chanel began to market a product that today is part of a global market that is estimated to be worth $7.5 billion a year: perfume.

In 1925, Chanel launched her first perfume, No. 5, which was a mixture of over eighty ingredients blended by the chemist Ernest Beaux who owned a labouratory in Grasse, the sacred home of the French perfume industry. Beaux was at the forefront of the developments of synthetic perfumes using aldehydes to enhance the fragrance of costly, natural ingredients such as jasmine. Chanel was not the first *couturier* to diversify into perfume: Paul Poiret was first in 1912 with a scent named after one of his daughters, Rosie, followed in 1923 by Madame Lanvin with Arpege. However, Chanel was the first to put a *couturier*'s name on the bottle. Chanel No. 5 has become the most successful designer perfume with sales of over 10 million bottles per year. And we continue to buy it despite the fact that the ingredients cost an estimated $3 (c. £2), the packaging an estimated $6 (c. £4), advertising $8 (c. £5) and administration $8 (c. £5) per 7ml bottle, which carries a trade price of around $35 (c. £20). A 60 per cent mark-up brings the retail price close to $70

Calvin Klein's Obsession, first marketed in 1985. Like Klein's jeans campaigns, the advertising deliberately employed erotic associations which generated huge media atttention, in turn guaranteeing the perfume's success.

(c. £40): ounce per ounce about the same price as gold. And we will carry on buying even after we know these facts because designer perfumes offer us the most affordable entry route into the fantasy lifestyle.

Perfumes have become a lucrative sideline for designers because they provide a marketable and affordable signature which reaches huge audiences world-wide. Chanel's venture into perfumes was to be widely copied: the shelves are full of fragrances that have survived the market launch and have

endured the test of time: Each year, 80–90 new perfumes are launched: after three years, only 20–25 will still be around. Calvin Klein's Obsession, first marketed in 1985, has been perhaps the most controversial new perfume, though not for its scent. Not only did the perfume's name 'disturb' but the marketing techniques used deliberately employed erotic associations, which generated huge media attention and guaranteed the success of the scent. Furthermore, the Obsession campaign addressed both women and men. Since the 1980s, the sales of men's perfumes has risen steadily and the new scents stressed 'active masculinity' through their advertising and their names, for example, like Ralph Lauren's Polo. Many others are quite happy to apply names like L'Homme, Pour Homme and Uomo next to the designer's signature.

There are few products left in the world that many designers have not considered putting their names to. Apart from designer diapers and coffins we can probably go from the cradle to the grave wearing designer-label, ready-to-wear, diffusion clothing and accessories.

RETAILING

The crucial link between the fashion industry and the consumer is retailing. No matter how much the designer is applauded at the end of the show and no matter how much the fashion editor 'loved it', ultimate success in the fashion business is achieved at retailing level by consumer acceptance of fashion measured in purchases. That low-cut, off-the-shoulder, backless, see-through crop-top may have looked terrific on Naomi and Christy on the catwalk, but who will really buy it?

Ever since people began producing goods surplus to personal consumption, trading has taken place; retailing is as old as recorded history itself, if not older. Many of our modern stores had their ancestors in ancient Greece and Rome and there have always been traders and pedlars travelling the world to buy and sell. Today, the retailing scene is still marked by the same global marketing and global retailing trend. European companies such as Laura Ashley in Great Britain, Benetton in Italy and Escada in West Germany have found the US market attractive and have opened retail stores in America. In 1991,

Fendi's 20,000 square feet of prime Fifth Avenue real estate became the largest European designer-owned store in New York City. Meanwhile, European markets have enticed American designers and companies with names like The Gap and Esprit opening retail stores in Britain and Germany, while in Japan, Brooks Brothers have more than 30 free-standing or in-store shops.

In the United States today it is estimated that there are more than two million retailing establishments, and of these, from mail-order firms and door-to-door selling operations to the latest in in-store boutiques and vertical shopping malls, 12 per cent are devoted to retailing fashion. Tokyo's Roppongi and Harajuki districts are testament to this world-wide trend: here there are more fashion stores than in any other city in the world. In Britain, former Arts Minister Lord Gowrie, in a speech at the London Business School, informed listeners that shopping was a legitimate late twentieth-century cultural pursuit.

Following mergers, acquisitions and, in the 1980s particularly, through leveraged buy-outs (LBOs), the classification of retail fashion

The interior of Gianni Versace's store, with its marble, glass and columns more usuallyfound in museums or palaces, serves to enforce the idea that *haute couture* is not only part of our history, but aspires to high culture.

stores has become increasingly complex as they have evolved in structure and organization. While traditionally an acquistion was paid for with cash or stock, the purchase price in an LBO is often 90 per cent borrowed money. In other words, the new owners may control the business while putting up less than 10 per cent of the purchase price. In order to repay the debt, the new owners either sell off parts of the company or undertake harsh cost-cutting measures in order to improve the company's profits. In the

Burberry of London, manufacturers of the famous raincoats, have recently shed their old fashioned image by introducing younger fashions and sportswear under the Thomas Burberry label.

1980s, LBOs were often instigated by real estate developers who purchased retailers for the land and building values or break-up and resale value.

Retail stores, usually of equal size, can merge to pool resources, but in other instances, larger companies buy smaller ones that are similar but non-competing. For example, The Limited also owns Victoria's

Secret; Marks & Spencer owns Brooks Brothers, and catalogue retailer Spiegel are owned by Otto Versand, the largest mail-order business in Europe.

For many people however, three kinds of retailing outlets dominate their shopping experiences: department stores, speciality stores and mass merchandisers. Yet even these categories will overlap and recombine as nonstore-based retailing such as mail order and tele-shopping become more widespread.

Before the Industrial Revolution in Britain, the making of clothing was firmly based in the home; new clothes were made as and when they were needed and could be afforded. By the late eighteenth century and early nineteenth century, ready-made clothes began to appear in special 'show shops' in urban centres. As towns and cities grew and factories began to produce more goods in quantity, networks of retail merchants developed.

THE ARRIVAL OF THE DEPARTMENT STORE

There is no one inventor of the department-store concept: the origins of this form of retailing can be traced to several developments in Europe and America in the 1830s. Surprisingly, one of the first department stores did not even open in a capital city: Bainbridge's of Newcastle was set up in 1838 and by 1849 had 23 departments. Around the same period, Bon Marché of Paris, Jolly of Bath and Kendal Milne of Manchester were established, followed closely by Lord and Taylor's in New York and Marshall Field in Chicago. By 1900, almost all the familiar names were around, although not all were at their present addresses. Marshall and Snelgrove, Harrod's, Liberty's, Dickens and Jones and Whiteley's of Bayswater were amongst the most fashionable shops in London at the turn of the century. In 1909, Selfridge's on Oxford

Street, to a fanfare of trumpets, opened its doors on 130 departments, rest rooms, restaurants and window displays that were lit up at night.

Despite these exciting adventures in retailing, the production of fashionable clothes was still largely in the hands of the Paris *couture* houses. The only alternative was provided by American and European dressmaking and tailoring firms who bought the sketches or originals of Paris models along with the fabrics and produced 'reproductions' for their wealthier clients.

Towards the end of the nineteenth century however, a few of the more exclusive city stores such as Marshall Field in Chicago, B. Altman in New York and, in London, Selfridge's, Harrods and Liberty's, began custom dressmaking and sending buyers overseas to purchase the latest French fashions. Many of the department stores whose names today are synonymous with fashion built their reputation on these new custom salons where the wealthy could order fashionable garments of good quality fabrics and workmanship; for many years, custom-made clothes remained an important aspect of department-store retailing. However, by the 1970s, the growing and continually improving ready-to-wear industry would see the demise of the custom operations in department stores.

A department store in the United States today is defined by the Bureau of the Census as a retail establishment that employs at least 25 people and sells three categories of general

The most famous shop in London, Harrods claims to be the largest department store in Europe. Advertising in the 1970s informed us that we could 'Enter a different world'; contemporary advertising reminds us that 'There is only one Harrods'.

merchandise: apparel and accessories, home furnishings and household items. Seibu in Japan claims to be the biggest department store in the world, Harrod's in Knightsbridge, the largest in Europe while Macy's in New York is the largest in the US. Yet size or tradition is no guarantee of success: in the 1950s on Kensington High Street in London there were no fewer than four department stores, now only one remains.

SHOPS WITHIN SHOPS

As consumer credit is squeezed even tighter in the 1990s, the top department stores throughout the world in order to survive in a fiercely competitive market have followed the American pattern of 'shops within shops' where clothes are arranged according to designer labels. These in-store units can either be leased departments or designer boutiques. With the former, many department stores have leased floor space to outside organizations who are better equipped to handle a special line. Often customers are not even aware that these leased departments are owned, merchandised and staffed by outside companies rather than the department store itself. The most commonly leased departments are beauty salons, furs, fine jewellery, shoes and bridal wear.

The in-store boutique

The term 'in-store designer boutique' refers to a permanent location and square footage of space within the store for the sole purpose of displaying only that designer's or manufacturer's merchandise. The in-store boutique allows manufacturers to present their collections as a unified whole, without the store buyers' 'editing' the range and also allows the opportunity for garments to be merchandised according to the designer's or manufacturer's concepts rather than the department store's ideas. For this reason it has been common for the vendor to supply the fixtures and fittings of the in-store boutique. For example, Ralph Lauren's Polo boutiques are fitted with the wooden accessories which continue the visual style of the Polo 'mother shops' to a wider market. Both leasing and in-store boutiques have offered customers all the advantages of one-stop department-store shopping as well as, for many, the opportunity to buy fashions without entering the exclusive and rarified atmosphere of some free-standing boutiques. Many consumers prefer to enter shops where they can see other people shopping. But what the in-store boutique cannot offer the customer is that very thing prized by many: the shopping bag with the designer's name emblazoned on it. In leased departments or in-store boutiques you will find your clothes packaged in the department store's own bags.

Private label merchandising

Exclusivity has long been an aspect of a fashion store's uniqueness and a major selling point for many a fashion victim. Yet as department stores stock more, exclusivity decreases and all stores start to look the same. To counter this trend and encourage customer loyalty, department stores have devised 'private label' merchandise lines which often carries the store's name alongside the name of the designer on the label. These private label garments have been manufactured directly for the department store to their specifications. Some department stores now have in-house design teams to develop private label merchandise while others continue to send their buyers to purchase popular items in Europe and have them copied in Asia.

Speciality stores

As marketing becomes increasingly segmented, speciality stores have often taken the lead in fashion retailing. These stores carry one category or related categories of fashion merchandise and cater to a particular kind of customer and provide a more personalized service. Some speciality stores may cater only for men, or women or children – the 'designer baby' shop Oilily is a good example. With acknowledgement that not all women are of catwalk-model proportions but still have the right to look good, some speciality shops cater for either 'petite' sizes or 'lavish' figures.

In London, international speciality fashion shops include Brown's, which runs, in addition to the shops at numbers 23 to 27 South Molton Street, Labels for Less and the Romeo Gigli and G Gigli shops on the same street, with the Comme des Garçons shop nearby. Other British speciality fashion stores include Whistles, Joseph and Next, while in the US the leading fashion speciality stores include Barney's, Bergdorf Goodman, Saks Fifth Avenue, The Gap, The Limited, Neiman Marcus of Dallas, I. Magnin of San Francisco and Bullocks Wilshire of Los Angeles. In continental Europe however, the speciality stores retailing fashion largely remain the traditional designer-owned shops in Paris, Milan, Florence and Rome.

In addition to the trends in 'deep niche' retailing – stores such as Sock Shop, Knickerbox and Tie Rack in Britain and The Forgotten Woman in New York (which offers fashions in larger sizes) that cater to very specific consumer demands – there is a new trend for large speciality stores to expand by adding superstores like Limited Express on Madison Avenue New York. Many designers and manufacturers have moved towards vertical marketing which allows them to control their products from concept to consumer by selling their goods in company-owned stores. While this has always been the usual arrangement in France and Italy where designers have always had their boutiques, for others it is a new venture. Some companies like The Gap are retailers that

Saks Fifth Avenue is a leader in private label merchandise which carries both the store and designer's name.

have expanded into manufacturing, while manufacturers like Anne Klein, Liz Claiborne and Esprit have opened their own retail outlets.

Groups, chainstores and franchises

With both department stores and speciality stores, there are two kinds of multiple-unit retail organizations: groups and chainstores. The distinctions between them are largely

organizational: most department stores are members of group organizations consisting of the mother store with multiple branches. Examples of these in Britain have included Burton's which owns or has owned Debenham's, Top Shop, Top Man, Principles, Principles for Men, Evans, Dorothy Perkins and Harvey Nichols. In a chain organization, the stores are basically uniform as they are all merchandised from a central office. Some chains have become huge retailers – The Gap has added Gap Kids and, most recently, Gap Baby. In Britain, Next have over 400 stores and Laura Ashley, the leader in this trend, has more than 450 shops world-wide. No longer then is the term 'chain store' associated only with cut-price merchandise.

A further option in retailing is available through franchising where retailing companies sell the rights to retail their merchandise. Manufacturers like this kind of deal because their products are sold under a well-known brand name and merchandised according to the 'designers' specifications which helps to protect their image. Retailers benefit because they are guaranteed stock and the right to use the brand name in advertising. But the store has no say in what it takes from the line: it must carry whatever merchandise is sent to them from the manufacturer, whether they want it or not. Some of the Mondi shops (a German manufacturer) in Europe and the US are franchises as are many Body Shops and French Connection shops; while they claim that they do not franchise, Benetton's operations are very similar. While the advantages for the manufacturer and retailer are clear, for the customer it is more complicated as the 'global designs' of these companies cannot take account of regional or national variations in culture, tradition or even the weather. Perhaps the purchase of a new raincoat is what is required, rather than the floral or tropical motif skirt offered at all the franchised shops.

Mass merchandising and malls

The third category of retailing belongs to the mass merchants who provide the shopper with commodity merchandise – those standard basics – often in a department-store format. These companies really put the mass into mass merchandise: Sears (with 825 stores), K-Mart and Wal-Mart are the US giants. Marks & Spencer is Britain's largest retailer with more sales per square foot of selling space than any other store in the

Trump Tower in New York, part of the growing trend in shopping malls.

Rodeo Drive, Beverly Hills: synonymous with fashion

world, while Germanys' C & A has also earned the reputation for providing affordable, fashionable clothing.

Most of the world's top retail stores began in the major marketing centres and still today, certain streets or areas of cities have become synonymous with shopping for fashion. Fifth Avenue in New York, the Union Square area in San Francisco and Rodeo Drive in Beverly Hills fly the flag for fashion in the US, while in London, Oxford Street, Bond Street, Knightsbridge and Covent Garden fashion stores compete to separate shoppers from their cash. In many cities in both Britain and the US, the malls have added to the range of retailing environments: Trump Tower and the A & S Plaza in New York, The San Francisco Center with its spiral escalators which cost nearly half a million dollars (c. £312,500) each per floor, and in Britain, the Metro Centre at Gateshead and Lakeside at Thurrock, are just a few examples. But these are mere babies compared to the giant 5.2 million square feet of climate-controlled retail selling spaces, theatres, miniature golf courses, amusement park and 110 acres of landscape gardens to bring the outside world inside, but under the strict control of the West Edmonton Mall in Alberta, Canada.

The glittering prizes: a department store can not offer are that ultimate trophy signifying a successful shopping trip: the designer name shopping bag!

MAIL ORDER

With all the attractions of shopping in giant malls or in the designer boutiques of the fashion capitals of the world, some feared that the death knell would be tolled for the remaining traditional mail-order business companies. Yet a surprising number of people who either hate travelling to the city or do not have the time or money to do so, find it more convenient to browse through catalogues and to have the merchandise they have selected sent straight to their own front doors. In 1989 *Newsweek* reported that catalogue mailings increased in the US from 5.8 billion in 1980 to 12.4 billion copies in 1988. Apparel catalogue retailers today include Grattan's, Freeman's, Empire Stores, L.L. Bean, Lands End Spiegel and Otto Versand, the largest mail-order company in Europe. But all retailers have now realized that mail-order services bring them increased businesses and many have added a catalogue or directory 'arm' to their business.

In the United States, dedicated shopaholics have joined the electronic superhighway. A number of on-line information services are now offering a shop-by-computer service: on the Prodigy System customers can selected from more than 50,000 separate items.

For the majority of shoppers, at least for the time being, it is the variety and quality of retail fashion stores that offer the most exciting venues for shopping and many now go out of their way to make parting with our hard-earned cash a most pleasurable experience by providing us with personal shopping services, designer coffee bars and most thoughtfully, 'crèche areas' for 'adult males'. It is now possible for men to wait in a safe, often supervised environment enjoying televised sports and reading motoring magazines while their wives and girlfriends get down to the really serious business of searching for that certain something that will complete her wardrobe.

READING LIST

Ash, Juliet and Wilson, Elizabeth, *Chic Thrills*, Pandora, 1992

Brush Kidwell, Claudia and Steele, Valerie, *Men and Women*: *Dressing the Part*, Smithsonian Institution Press, 1989

Coleridge, Nicholas, *The Fashion Conspiracy*: *A Remarkable Journey Through the Empires of Fashion*, Mandarin, 1988

Davis, Fred, *Fashion, Culture and Identity*, University of Chicago Press, 1992

De Marly, Diana, *The History of Haute Couture*, B.T Batsford Ltd, 1980

Drew, Linda, *The Business of Fashion*, Cambridge University Press, 1992

Ewing, Elizabeth, *History of 20th Century Fashion*, B. T. Batsford Ltd, 1974, 1987

Gross, Michael, Model: *The Ugly Business of Beautiful Women*, Bantam Press, 1995

Jarnow, Jeannette A., Judelle, Beatrice and Guereiro, Miriam, *Inside the Fashion Business*: *Texts and Readings*, John Willey and Sons, 1981

Laver, James, *Costume*, Cassell, 1963

McDermott, Catherine, *Street Style*, Design Council, 1987

McDowell, Colin, Diectory of 20th Century Fashion,

Miller, Lesley, *Cristóbal Balenciaga*, B.T. Batsford Ltd, 1993

Steele, Valerie, *Women of Fashion*, Rizzoli, 1991

Tomlinson, A., *Consumption, Identity and Style*, R.K.P., 1990

Widdows, Lee and McGuinness, Jo, *Catwalk: Working with Models*, B.T. Batsford Ltd, 1996

Wilson, Elizabeth, *Adorned in Dreams: Fashion and Modernity*, Virago, 1985

Wilson, Elizabeth and Taylor, Lou, *Through the Looking Glass*, BBC Books, 1989

York, Peter, *Style Wars*, Sedgwick and Jackson, 1980

SELECTED LIST OF DESIGNERS

Armani, Giorgio 1935-

Balenciaga, Cristobal 1895-1972

Beene, Geoffrey 1927-

Cardin, Pierre 1922-

Carnegie, Hattie 1889-1956

Cashin, Bonnie 1915-

Cerutti, Nino 1930-

Chanel, Gabrielle 'Coco' 1883-1971

Courreges, Andre 1923-

Dior, Christian 1905-1957

Fath, Jacques 1912-1954

Fendi (Adele Fendi) 1897-1978

Fortuny, Mariano 1871-1949

Galliano, John 1960-

Gaultier, Jean Paul 1952-

Givenchy, Hubert 1927-?

Gres, Alix 1910-?

James, Charles 1960-

Karan, Donna 1948-

Kawakubo, Rei 1942-

Klein, Calvin 1942-

Lagerfeld, Karl 1939-

Lauren, Ralph 1939-

McCardell, Claire 1905-58

Miyake, Issey 1935-

Muir, Jean 1933-1995

Patou, Jean 1887-1936

Poiret, Paul 1879-1944

Quant, Mary 1934-

Ricci, Nina 1883-1970

Saint Laurent, Yves 1936-

Schiaparelli, Elsa 1890-1973

Ungaro, Emmanuel 1933-

Valentino 1932-

Versace, Gianni 1946-97

Vionnet, Madeleine 1876-1975

Westwood, Vivienne 1941-

Yamamoto, Yohji 1943-

PICTURE ACKNOWLEDGEMENTS

7 **BT Batsford Picture Archive**; 8 **Frank Spooner Pictures**; 9 **Frank Spooner Pictures**; 11 **Rex Features**;

12 **Rex Features**; 13 **Rex Features**; 14 **Frank Spooner Pictures**; 17 **Fashion Research Centre, Bath**;

18 **Advertising Archive**; 19 **Niall McInerney**; 20 **Advertising Archive**; 21 **Advertising Archive**;

24 **Advertising Archive**; 27 **Advertising Archive**; 28 **Niall McInerney**; 30 **Niall McInerney**; 31 **Rex Features**;

32 **Niall McInerney**; 34 **Rex Features**; 36 **Frank Spooner Pictures**; 39 **Advertising Archive**; 40 **Rex Features**;

43 **Rex Features**; 44 **Frank Spooner**; 45 **Rex Features**; 47 **Rex Features**; 49 **Nlall McInerney**;

51 & 52 **Joel Finler Collection**; 53 **Joel Finler Collection**; 54 **Joel Finler Collection**; 56 **Joel Finler Collection**;

57 **Niall McInerney**; 58 **Joel Finler Collection**; 59 **Joel Finler Collection**; 61 **Rex Features**; 63 (top) **Rex Features**;

63 (bottom) **Rex Features**; 65 **Rex Features**; 67 **Rex Features**; 68 **Rex Features**; 71 **Niall McInerney**;

73 **Rex Features**; 75 **Rex Features**; 76. & 79 **Advertising Archive**; 77 **Rex Features**; 81 **Rex Features**; 82 **Rex Features**; 84 **Rex Features**; 87 **Rex Features**; 88 **Rex Features**; 89 **Rex Features**; 90 **Rex Features**.

Front: Frank Spooner Pictures
Back: Hulton Getty

INDEX